Consecrating the World

On Mundane Liturgical Theology

David W. Fagerberg

Consecrating the World

*On Mundane
Liturgical Theology*

Angelico Press

First published
by Angelico Press 2016
© David W. Fagerberg 2016

For information, address:
Angelico Press
4709 Briar Knoll Dr.
Kettering, OH 45429
angelicopress.com

978-1-62138-168-6 (pbk)
978-1-62138-169-3 (ebook)

Cover image: modified from dome fresco, baptistery,
Zica monastery, Serbia, 13th–14th century
Cover design: Michael Schrauzer

To Fr. Boguslaw Migut,
The John Paul II Catholic University, Lublin, Poland

With thanks for friendship
and fruitful discussions about liturgy and spirituality

Is it surprising that a Church that is Catholic
should find for me someone of like mind from another land?

CONTENTS

Preface

THE EASTERN CHRISTIAN ascetical tradition has described the sinner's malady as disordered faculties called passions—what the Western moral tradition has dealt with under the category of the vices. The passions are cured in a sinner by grace stimulating the sinner's ascetical battle with them, and the saint's joy is a freedom from the passions and the raising of the natural virtues and instilling of the theological virtues. Philosophy has noticed the benefits that asceticism offers to a person, but its primary purpose is the greater glorification of God, which is something that only Christianity fully understands. Therefore, even though some of the ascetical disciplines look the same when practiced by a Stoic philosopher or a Christian, by Marcus Aurelius or St. Basil, it would seem that the asceticism is different by motive and end. I have therefore called that asceticism which capacitates a person for liturgy "liturgical asceticism." It has a supernatural end, its source and telos come from beyond the heavens. It joins the Son of God in his *kenosis* and his ascension, and its pathway is through the door of the Paschal mystery of cross and resurrection.

I have written about this in my book *On Liturgical Asceticism.* What I have been able to do now is to take a step further back and think about the effect this liturgical asceticism would have outside the sanctuary and nave of the Church. This was made possible by lectures delivered in 2014–15. Chapters one, four, and five were delivered at the University of St. Mary of the Lake/Mundelein Seminary as the Paluch Lectures of that year, and I am grateful for the opportunity to return to this special place and visit dear friends again. A shorter version of chapter three, and with slightly different content, was delivered at the Pontifical University of the Holy Cross (Santa Croce) in Rome during a conference in March 2015. I'm grateful to them for permission to use this expanded version here.

This book may therefore be considered a companion volume to

my study on liturgical asceticism, but it cannot really be considered "Volume II" because it does not continue on exactly the same trajectory. And yet the two books are connected. So I imagine them as two panels of a diptych, and the hinge that holds them together is a single quotation from Charles Williams. In his study of the figure of Beatrice in the *Divine Comedy* he describes Dante meeting an angel with two keys, one silver and one gold. Williams says they reflect two methods, one of Rejection, the other of Affirmation. "Rejection is a silver key, which is 'more dear'; Affirmation is a golden key, more difficult to use. Yet both are necessary, for any life."[1] The thesis of my diptych is that liturgical asceticism is conditional for a liturgical cosmos. Liturgical asceticism capacitates a person for liturgy. The preliminary, negative asceticism is only to clear out the silt, to awaken the sleepwalker, to dust off the coin that bears the king's image, so that the *imago Dei* can again stand aright, and offer the holy oblation in peace. And where is this sacrificial oblation accomplished? In both the sacred and the profane. It happens in the former under sensible signs, and it happens in the latter by *consecratio mundi*. The sacramental liturgy and our personal liturgy are connected as in a seamless garment.

I do not find the phrase *consecratio mundi* used much anymore, but Pope Paul VI did when he wanted to describe lay men and women as the world's perfect citizen ("Layman Should Be World's Perfect Citizen," General Audience of April, 1969). One of the effects of the Council now pervading the life of the Church, he said, was to give the honor of teaching Christian doctrine to expressions, which, though they existed prior to the Council, have now entered into everyday use and taken on characteristic meanings. "One of these expressions is '*consecratio mundi*,' the consecration of the world. These words have distant roots, but the merit of having made them particularly expressive in connection with the apostolate of the laity rests with Pius XII of venerated memory."[2] (Indeed, he finds it in his predecessor in half a dozen addresses.) Paul VI thinks the key to its meaning lies in what

---

1. Charles Williams, *The Figure of Beatrice: A Study in Dante* (New York: The Noonday Press, 1961), 157.

2. http://www.ewtn.com/library/PAPALDOC/P6LAYMAN.HTM.

it means to consecrate. "Let it suffice here to recall that by consecration we mean, not the separation of a thing from what is profane in order to reserve it exclusively, or particularly, for the Divinity, but, in a wider sense, the re-establishment of a thing's relationship to God according to its own order, according to the exigency of the nature of the thing itself, in the plan willed by God."

To consecrate the world is to reestablish it in its proper relationship to God, along with every single thing in it. This is the priestly activity for which Adam and Eve were created, which they forfeited, and which the New Adam has given to the Church, his New Eve. Because of their secular vocation, the laity are in a position to do this, as *Lumen Gentium* has said:

> But the laity, by their very vocation, seek the kingdom of God by engaging in temporal affairs and by ordering them according to the plan of God. They live in the world, that is, in each and in all of the secular professions and occupations. They live in the ordinary circumstances of family and social life, from which the very web of their existence is woven. They are called there by God that by exercising their proper function and led by the spirit of the Gospel they may work for the sanctification of the world from within as a leaven. (*Lumen Gentium* ¶31)

This will involve rescuing things from their bondage—an action called exorcism. Exorcism reclaims something for its original purpose. What was the original purpose of the cosmos?

It is appropriate to especially associate consecration with the Holy Spirit; therefore, I have conceived these chapters around the Dove. The first chapter concerns the affirmation of images made possible by the descent of the Dove; the second chapter understands eschatology as the background melody to the world that we can hear with the ear of the Dove; the third chapter wonders how we may be taken aloft on the wing of the Dove; the fourth chapter recalls Gregory of Nyssa saying that the baptized see with the eye of the Dove; and the fifth chapter concerns mimicking the sacrificial voice of the Dove.

If a thing were reestablished in its relationship to God, then man and woman would be doing their task as cosmic priests. If all things were reestablished in their relationship to God, then the liturgy would reach out from the sacred into the profane, from the Church into the world, from the ritual into life. Robert Taft has said that "The purpose of all Christian liturgy is to express in a ritual moment that which should be the basic stance of every moment of our lives."[3] We express in action what should be the activity of our heart, and that means that what we see in the ritual liturgy is something that should be going on within our lives constantly. The liturgy—that whirlwind of heaven—would make its appearance not only in the sacraments but in our person. It should be an example of what I am here calling *mundane liturgical theology*: liturgical theology of our life in the world.[4] *Mundanus*: "worldly; of/belonging to the world." Christ stooped down in the Incarnation in order to put his shoulder under the human race and lift us up. Christ descends to his people in the liturgy in order to lift us up to God. How does that work? That is my question. So the five chapters discern a world of affirmation, an eschatological world, a mystical world, a world that is sacramental, and a world that is sacrificial. I know that liturgy is the public ceremony of the Church, but it does not exist for its own sake any more than does the gospel. They both have a mission orientation, because they are both charged with a power of transfiguration. Thus it was that my teacher, Aidan Kavanagh, used to regularly say in class that "liturgy is doing the world the way the world was meant to be done."[5]

That is the liturgy we would like to talk about in this book.

DECEMBER, 2015
FEAST OF THE IMMACULATE CONCEPTION

---

3. Robert Taft, "Sunday in the Eastern Tradition," *Beyond East and West: Problems in Liturgical Understanding* (Washington, DC: The Pastoral Press, 1984), 32.

4. And what Orthodox priest Ion Bria called "the liturgy after the liturgy." See his *The Liturgy after the Liturgy: Mission and Witness from an Orthodox Perspective* (Geneva: World Council of Churches, 1996). Also in article form, "The Liturgy After the Liturgy," *International Review of Mission*, 67 [265] (1978): 86–90.

5. "A liturgy of Christians is thus nothing less than the way a redeemed world is, so to speak, done." Aidan Kavanagh, *On Liturgical Theology* (New York: Pueblo Publishing Company, 1984), 100. And "What one witnesses in the liturgy is the world being done as the world's Creator and Redeemer will the world to be done," from Kavanagh, *Elements of Rite* (New York: Pueblo Publishing Company, 1982), 46.

1

The Descent of the Dove

THE LITURGY is not a simple object to look at. I mean that it is a complex object we want to examine here. We can focus our eyes to either look *at* liturgy or to look *through* liturgy. Much of liturgical studies does the former: it looks at liturgy's surface to notice its rubrics, sacramentaries, structure, ceremonies, architecture, etc. But I am here proposing that we can look through liturgy to notice... what? What is one invited to see through a liturgical lens? What sights does the liturgical lens make possible? To what things does liturgy have relevance? My intention in what follows is to answer, "Everything." Liturgical insight is required to see into the cosmos, history, the *polis*, mankind, earth's matter, heaven's empyrean, man and woman as cosmic priests—everything. Why food? To eat. Why violin? Music. Why something instead of nothing? Liturgy.[1]

There stands a consecrated temple—let us walk through it. What do we see? An altar, a font, statues and images, two stages for action (a sanctuary and a nave). What is it for? Its design and furnishings make it a poor office, a poor bank, a poor home; we could not understand the purpose of the building if we did not know it was built for liturgy. There stands another temple, the cosmological temple, the world—let us walk through it. What do we see? Spirit and matter, creatures capable of speech and sign, angels and animals and embodied souls, heaven and earth seeking connection. What is it for? If we did not know it was built for liturgy, we would have as much trouble understanding its purpose as we had understanding

1. Liturgy gives teleology to ontology.

5

the stone temple. Liturgical cosmology is the keystone of the doctrine of creation.

This insight does not come easily. We do not see into the interior heart of creation without a cost, because the sons of Adam and daughters of Eve are afflicted with a sinful myopia. (*Myein*—to shut; *ops*—eye; we have become too nearsighted to see transcendence.) Among the many consequences of our race's original sin are included eyes that were designed to see by the light of heaven but are now dimmed, needing renewal. The Son left the side of his Father and entered our history, our world, our humanity precisely for this renewal, and embedded the Holy Spirit in his sacramental body to accomplish this for any who desire and permit it. The initial step is called conversion and the completed step is called holiness, a seed faithfully sown in this life to be reaped beatifically in the next, which conforms us to God and capacitates us to participate in the life of the Trinity. Liturgy is the perichoresis of the Trinity kenotically extended to invite our synergistic ascent into deification.[2] Liturgy is participation in the perichoresis of the Trinity; asceticism is the capacitation for that participation; theology is union with God, making the Church's liturgy an act of *theologia*; and liturgical asceticism is the life-long process of deification that results in the removal of the cataracts of sin from our eyes, giving us clear sight, at last.

What would the world look like with these cataracts removed? What if we could encounter objects in the world not as temptations but as sacramental gifts by which we could glorify God? We would still have to be on guard against the passions, but we could nevertheless experience the world anew. Charles Williams suggests our bipolar state by describing Dante's encounter with an angel holding two keys. The keys have been associated with the sacrament of penance, and no doubt, he says, they are:

> But it has another allusiveness. The keys are also the methods of Rejection and Affirmation. Rejection is a silver key, which is "more

2. My definition of liturgy in *On Liturgical Asceticism* (Washington, DC: The Catholic University of America Press, 2013), 9.

dear"; Affirmation is a golden key, more difficult to use. Yet both are necessary, for any life. . . . The Church is not a way for the soul to escape hell but to become heaven; it is virtues rather than sins which we must remember.[3]

Since Williams has planted the metaphor, I am going to let him further explain it, along with two authors who influenced him, one lateral and one anterior, viz., C. S. Lewis and Coventry Patmore.

In my earlier book I tested the silver key; here I wish to test the golden one. The purpose of the ascetical silver key of rejection is to make it possible for us to turn the mundane golden key of affirmation. A mundane liturgical theology will examine how to do the world the way the world was meant to be done. This will require looking at the world through corrective lenses to repair our myopia. It will require seeing the mundane by the light of Mount Tabor that streams forth from the altar, through the nave, out the narthex upon our daily life. The thread of mundane theology is stretched tautly between the two poles of protology and eschatology, from our alpha to our omega.

Two launch keys are required. The desert ascetic, who has left the world, and the mundane ascetic, who is still in the world but not of it, cooperate because the key of negation and the key of affirmation must co-operate the lock. The desert ascetic renounces the world in order to sharpen his wanting, and finds his wanting to be his having. The mundane ascetic finds his wanting sharpened by what he has as the world takes him by the hand, sacramentally, and leads him to its Creator. In his history of the Holy Spirit, *The Descent of the Dove*, Williams writes,

> Both methods, the Affirmative Way and the Negative Way, were to co-exist; one might almost say, to co-inhere, since each was to be the key of the other: in intellect as in emotion, in morals as in doctrine. . . . The one Way was to affirm all things orderly until the universe throbbed with vitality; the other to reject all things until there was nothing anywhere but He. The Way of Affirmation was

---

3. Williams, *The Figure of Beatrice: A Study in Dante*, 157.

to develop great art and romantic love and marriage and philosophy and social justice; the Way of Rejection was to break out continually in the profound mystical documents of the soul, the records of the great psychological Masters of Christendom. All was involved in Christendom, and between them, as it were, hummed the web of the ecclesiastical hierarchy, laboring, ordering, expressing, confirming, and often misunderstanding, but necessary to any organization in time.[4]

Although both keys are required, there is an antecedence to the silver key, for until we are freed from the passions we will not be able to do the world righteously. But this makes the golden key, the one that is more difficult to use, more dear. This silver key must be turned first, but the golden key turns out to be the *raison d'être* for asceticism. The end directs the means, the telos directs our discipline, heaven directs our escape from hell, the virtues direct our battle against the vices. Left to itself, the way of negation could easily become masochistic, puritanical, and (as Williams said) we would become satisfied with escaping hell, but not becoming heaven. Our failure is lack of desire, and the only sorrow is not being a saint. We misunderstand Christianity if we dabble in it as a sort of pacifying morality that does not maintain the tension within us that could launch us toward heaven. Gregory of Nyssa observed how water spreads itself out in all directions unless it is contained, but water that is contained within a pipe will often burst upward because of the force of the pressure. "It does this against its natural downward motion because it has nowhere else to flow. So, too, is it with the mind of man. If it is confined on all sides by the water-tight pipe of chastity, if it has no other outlets, it will be raised up by the very tendency of its motion towards a love of higher things."[5] The tendency of our human motion is not neutered, it is elevated. The

4. Charles Williams, *The Descent of the Dove* (London: The Religious Book Club, 1939), 56–58.

5. Gregory of Nyssa, *On Virginity*, ch. 6. This translation from Jean Daniélou, *From Glory to Glory: Texts from Gregory of Nyssa's Mystical Writings* (Crestwood, NY: St. Vladimir's Seminary Press, 1979), 103.

ascetical way of negation is restrictive for the sole purpose of pressuring us upward. It is that upward arc that we want to explore here.

What awakened Augustine from the spell of the Manicheans was seeing the parasitic nature of evil. Evil is not something; it is the lack of something, or the distortion of something. The relationship between good and evil is not commutative: subtract the good and you will get evil, but subtract the evil and you will not produce good. We must get our ontology straight, and avoid dualism. Were I in a bright room, I could produce darkness by subtracting light (block the windows, tape over the keyhole) because light is something and darkness is its absence; but were I in a cave, I could not produce light by subtracting darkness because darkness is not something, it is an absence. Gregory of Nyssa applies this ontological understanding to the vices and virtues. "For as sight is an activity of nature, and blindness a deprivation of that natural operation, such is the kind of opposition between virtue and vice. It is, in fact, not possible to form any other notion of the origin of vice than as the absence of virtue."[6] A virtue is something, and a vice is the absence of that virtue; but it does not work in reverse. What other origin could vice possibly have? It cannot come from the hand of God, who is good. And Satan is incapable of ontological product; he can only deceive and corrupt. Though it is convenient to make a side-by-side list of vices and virtues, this tidy organization should not fool us into thinking they are like two columns on a restaurant menu, from which we choose. A vice is where a virtue should be, but is not; a vice is a virtue in disorder; a vice is where a virtue should operate in a certain manner, but does not. There are not two things to choose between, darkness and light; light is, and darkness is its lack. Neither do we choose between a vice and a virtue, because a vice is where a virtue is lacking. Vainglory appears where humility declines, anger appears where meekness has failed, and gluttony appears where temperance is absent. Similarly, we do not choose between sin and deification, because sin is simply our failure to participate in the life of God that has been kenotically extended.

---

6. Gregory of Nyssa, *The Great Catechism*, chapter 5.

We see, then, how the two keys must work together. First a Rejection of Images so that we wake up, then a negation of our rejection —a double negative that produces a positive. By this Affirmation of Images we can virtuously affirm the truth, beauty, and goodness of the world. The whole world has the potential for being sacramental communication and sacrificial response, but for the problem of sin. That's why it is not enough for theology to talk about the world as sacrament; theology must also account for how the world can become sacrament for us sinners. Hence, liturgical asceticism. Before light can bring the color blue to our eye, our eye must be open and sound. Before the world can function sacramentally, our eye must be open and sound. The way of negation must precede the way of affirmation, cataract surgery must precede clear vision, and the way of liturgical asceticism must precede the way of mundane liturgical theology. But when the silver key has done its job, what can the golden key unlock for us?

Williams proposes that the great intellectual teacher of the Way of Rejection was Dionysius the Areopagite, who took theologians on an ascent through a renunciation of all images in order to lead us to God himself. Then Williams proposes that the Way of Affirmation has had many teachers, but its full expression had to wait for Dante. "It may be that that way could not be too quickly shown to the world in which the young Church lived. It was necessary first to establish the awful difference between God and the world before we could be permitted to see the awful likeness."[7] Chesterton made the same point when he described the Dark Ages as a period of purgation in which water itself was washed, and fire purified as by fire.[8] Only after the purgation of idolatry toward nature could man return to nature with safety.

Williams writes a book-length study that can be described as an epistemology of what impelled and guided Dante. Dante first knew love in Beatrice, and love is of God, even eros. Through Beatrice there springs forth in Dante a new quality, and Williams wants to

7. Williams, *The Figure of Beatrice*, 9.
8. G. K. Chesterton, *St. Francis of Assisi*, in *G. K. Chesterton: Collected Works*, Vol. 2 (San Francisco: Ignatius Press, 1986), 44.

analyze the origin and nature of that new quality. Since he calls the mystery Romance, he calls its analysis Romantic Theology:

> I keep the word Romantic for three reasons. The first is that there is no other word so convenient for describing that particular kind of sexual love. The second is that it includes other loves besides the sexual. The third is that in following the Dantean record of his love it may be possible to understand something more of Romanticism itself, and of its true and false modes of being. The word should not be too narrowly confined to a literary manner. It defines an attitude, a manner of receiving experience.[9]

Williams proposes that in the way Mystical Theology is theology applied to mystical experiences, and Dogmatic Theology is theology applied to thought about dogmas, so Romantic Theology is theology as applied to romantic experiences:

> The term does not imply, as will inevitably at first be thought, a theology based merely on fantasy and dream, concerning itself only with theological sentimentalities. It is a theology as exact as any other kind, but having for cause and subject those experiences of man which . . . are generally termed "romantic." The chief of these is romantic love; that is, sexual love between a man and a woman. . . . That there are other human experiences of this same far-reaching nature is undeniable—nature and friendship are perhaps the chief.[10]

The two ways of Negation and Affirmation may be symbolized, as the reader might already have guessed, by virginity and marriage. These two vocational states each symbolize one of the ways personally—i.e., symbolizes it in persons. Both Solovyov and Evdokimov

---

9. Williams, *The Figure of Beatrice*, 14.

10. Williams, *Outlines*, 7. Besides treating the theme in his three major books *The Figure of Beatrice*, *The Descent of the Dove*, and *He Came Down from Heaven*, Williams made it the topic of numerous articles, such as "Religion and Love in Dante: The Theology of Romantic Love," and a book he never published but was rescued from a single typed manuscript by Alice Mary Hadfield and published as *Outlines of Romantic Theology*.

say that there are two ascetical vocations, namely, monasticism and marriage. Every single baptized Christian has a vocation to asceticism, but there are two states of life in which that vocation is lived out within a publicly vowed commitment. The monk vows obedience and stability, the spouse vows unbreakable union, each connecting themselves to something beyond their solitary selves. The ascetical struggle against the passions is done cooperatively. A community is established that allows for outward expressions of love, but the mutual help must go further. Persons are bound together for the primary purpose of "forming and perfecting themselves in the interior life, so that through their partnership in life they may advance ever more and more in virtue, and above all that they may grow in true love toward God and their neighbor, on which indeed 'dependeth the whole Law and the Prophets.'" This remark comes not from a monastic rule, but from Pope Pius XI's encyclical on marriage.[11] If the desert accents the negative task of liturgical asceticism, the home accents the affirmative task of liturgical asceticism. Both flow from the cross through the ascetical channels of liturgical participation in Christ's offer of life in his death. So Williams says that just as every Mass was said once on Calvary, and at the Eucharist we are absorbed into that eternal offering, so each marriage was lived in Christ's life, and true lovers are absorbed into his eternity in their marriage:

> The principles of Romantic Theology can be reduced to a single formula: which is, the identification of love with Jesus Christ, and of marriage with His life. This again may be reduced to a single word—Immanuel. Everything else is modification and illustration of this. Romantic Theology, like the rest, is therefore first of all a Christology.... It is His manifestation of Himself in marriage which is the subject of Romantic Theology.[12]

Even though romantic sexual love is the preeminent expression of Romantic Theology, we have already heard Williams say that there are other human experiences that fall in this same class, chief

---

11. *Casti Connubii*, Encyclical of Pope Pius XI on Christian Marriage, 1930, ¶23.
12. Williams, *Outlines of Romantic Theology*, 14–15.

among them being nature and friendship. He can, therefore, give a broader definition of Romantic Theology when he puts it in more abstract terms. "It defines an attitude, a manner of receiving experience."[13] "Proper Romanticism neither denies nor conceals; neither fears nor flies. It desires only accuracy; 'look, look; attend.'"[14] One scholar interprets him as asserting that Romantic Theology is "the working out of ways in which an ordinary relationship between two people can become one that is extraordinary, one that grants us glimpses, visions of perfection."[15] Another interprets him as identifying a "strangeness flowering from the commonplace"; and yet another to mean "making the ordinary extraordinary."[16] But Williams stayed closer to the example of eros because he was working out the idea in conversation with Dante, so if we want to find a still fuller idea of Romance, we might do well to turn to C. S. Lewis.

Lewis greatly admired Williams, and the feeling was mutual; they first contacted each other by letter in 1936, and when Williams's office at Oxford University Press was moved to the city of Oxford, due to danger from bombing raids on London during the war, his friendship with Lewis was cemented in the famous meetings of the Inklings. Lewis credits Williams with inventing the category of Romantic Theology, and provides us an apt description of it in the preface to a collection of essays written by Williams's friends to honor him:

> He was a novelist, a poet, a dramatist, a biographer, a critic, and a theologian: a "romantic theologian" in the technical sense which he himself invented for those words. A romantic theologian does

---

13. Williams, *The Figure of Beatrice*, 14.

14. Ibid., 35.

15. Alice Mary Hadfield, introduction to *Outlines of Romantic Theology*, viii.

16. From Hadfield's introduction, viii; the first quote is attributed to John Buchan, the second is from Hadfield herself. She further adds, "For sex, love, and marriage are commonplace and ordinary; they can also and at the same time be strange and extraordinary. Romance, he felt, does not stand by itself; it is an aspect of the multiform relationship of men, women, and God, the study of which is theology's business. Romantic theology is, therefore, the working out of ways in which an ordinary relationship between two people can become one that is extraordinary, one that grants us glimpses, visions of perfection."

not mean one who is romantic about theology but one who is theological about romance, one who considers the theological implications of those experiences which are called romantic. The belief that the most serious and ecstatic experiences either of human love or of imaginative literature have such theological implications, and that they can be healthy and fruitful only if the implications are diligently thought out and severely lived, is the root principle of all his work.[17]

But Lewis had already been considering the fittingness of the term "Romance" when describing a feature in his own writing. In 1933, three years before he wrote to Williams and a dozen years before he wrote the above description, Lewis published the first book he wrote after his conversion to Christianity, *The Pilgrim's Regress*. And in a preface to the third edition from 1943, Lewis explains what kind of Romanticism he had in mind when he wrote it. There are seven ordinary definitions of "romantic," he says—stories about dangerous adventure, the marvelous, high-flown sentiments, the macabre, egoism, revolt against existing conventions, and sensibility to natural objects treated solemnly and enthusiastically—and then he flatly avows, "What I meant by Romanticism when I wrote *The Pilgrim's Regress* was not any one of these seven."[18] The subtitle of the book is *An Allegorical Apology for Christianity, Reason and Romanticism.* Romanticism has to do with desire awakened, but a special kind of desire, awakened in a special way, for a special end; that is why it cannot be understood in isolation from, or opposition to, Reason and Christianity.

What did Lewis mean, then? In a book of poems published when he was only 20 years old, *Spirits in Bondage*, Lewis gives voice to his

---

17. C. S. Lewis, preface to *Essays Presented to Charles Williams* (Grand Rapids, MI: Eerdmans Publishing Company, 1974), vi. Lewis edited this volume of collected essays written originally to present to Williams on his leaving Oxford, but as he died suddenly in 1945 it was published posthumously to honor him. There are essays by Lewis, Dorothy Sayers, J. R. R. Tolkien, Owen Barfield, Gervase Matthew, and Warnie Lewis.

18. Lewis, *The Pilgrim's Regress* (London: Fount Paperbacks, 1977), 10. The book was originally published in 1933, and this is from a preface added to the third edition of the book in 1943.

juvenile nihilistic belief that God has instilled deep desires in man that cannot be attained. At this point in his life he believed everyone would be bitterly disappointed if ever they thought they could reach the goal of their desire. He was leveling the accusation that had there been a God (he was still an atheist at this point), this God was mocking us by placing insatiable desires in our natures. Only after his conversion many years later could Lewis observe that "there are two kinds of longing. One is an askesis, a spiritual exercise, and the other is a disease."[19] The liturgical theology that rises from the face of the earth is a longing that itself can be an askesis. Because he had known both kinds he can be our guide to an askesis of longing, an Affirmation of Images. He discovered a desire that was not bitter, it was sweet even in its insatiability.

The sort of Romanticism that Lewis describes results in temporary disappointments, but not final disappointment, because disappointments are steps along a way of progress led by insatiable desire. Thus Romance is an experience of intense longing, but distinguished from other kinds of longings by two characteristics:

> In the first place, though the sense of want is acute and even painful, yet the mere wanting is felt to be somehow a delight. Other desires are felt as pleasures only if satisfaction is expected in the near future: hunger is pleasant only while we know (or believe) that we are soon going to eat. But this desire, even when there is no hope of possible satisfaction, continues to be prized, and even to be preferred to anything else in the world, by those who have once felt it. This hunger is better than any other fullness; this poverty better than all other wealth. And thus it comes about, that if the desire is long absent, it may itself be desired, and that new desiring becomes a new instance of the original desire.[20]

The second characteristic that identifies Romantic longing is that the object longed for is a mystery. Inexperienced people think they know what they are desiring, but Lewis believes they too often mis-

---

19. Lewis, "On Three Ways of Writing for Children," *Of Other Worlds: Essays and Stories* (New York: Harcourt, Inc., 1966), 30.
20. Lewis, *The Pilgrim's Regress*, preface, 12.

take an ectype for its archetype. He offers five examples of confusion, cases when one erroneously believes that if only one attained a certain object, then the desire would be satisfied: (i) A child looks at a hillside and wishes "if only I were there"; (ii) a person reads a tale or poem about forlorn lands and thinks he is wishing such places really existed; (iii) the person who experiences desire within the context of erotic suggestions believes he is desiring the perfect beloved; (iv) literature treats spirits with serious belief as if it anchors real magic; (v) studies of history or science confuse the desire with the intellectual craving for knowledge. Lewis responds,

> but every one of these impressions is wrong. The sole merit I claim for this book is that it is written by one who has proved them all to be wrong. . . . Every one of the supposed objects for the Desire is inadequate to it. An easy experiment will show that by going to the far hillside you will get either nothing, or else a recurrence of the same desire which sent you thither.[21]

The Pilgrim's Regress is a story of a desire that sends the protagonist John thither. One day John sees an Island, and his immediate, deep reaction is "I know now what I want."[22] The spring has been wound all at once, and its slow release is the plot of the remaining allegory. The sight of the Island prompts John to go from his country, his people, and his father's household to a land he does not know. (Abraham was pulled, not pushed.) But all sorts of other objects present themselves as ersatz satisfactions: brown girls with whom John fornicates, pseudo-sophisticates in the city of Claptrap, a more refined but nevertheless false love with Media Halfways, and siren songs of various kinds.

John's journey is only made possible by offering a two-sided resistance to attacks from opposite sides. To the materialist who says he should be satisfied with what he has managed to get, he replies "If it is what I wanted, why am I so disappointed when I get it?"[23] And to the puritan who says he should disdain and abandon the desire for

21. Ibid., 13–14.
22. Ibid., 34.
23. Ibid., 67.

the Island altogether because it always disappoints him, he replies "How can you say the Island is all bad when longing for the Island has brought me this far?"[24] *The Pilgrim's Regress* is not the story of a stoical puritan saving a wanton pagan, it is the story of a desirous pagan saving a deadened Pharisee! Indeed, John is paired with a traveling companion named Mr. Vertue whose problem is the opposite of John's. They are paired together in order to heal each other; both the moralist and the Romantic are inside Lewis. Mr. Vertue only travels because he has set himself a rule to do 30 miles a day, thinking that "the great thing is to have rules of some sort and to keep them,"[25] but by the end John must plead with him, "Vertue, give in. For once yield to desire. Have done with your choosing. *Want* something."[26] This want is Romance in action. It is being moved by desire. It is an Affirmation of the Image of the Island.

John must make a decision. Either he can say, as Lewis did in the poems of his youth, that desires are a nasty trick, instilled by a malicious God who, for all we know, may be entertained by our disappointments; or else he can say, as indeed he finally does, "What does not satisfy when we find it, was not the thing we were desiring."[27] Both the early and the late Lewis believe the desire to be insatiable, but to the early atheist that is sour and to the later believer that is sweet. Here is the same conclusion in Lewis's own voice in *Mere Christianity*:

> If I find in myself a desire which no experience in this world can satisfy, the most probable explanation is that I was made for another world. If none of my earthly pleasures satisfy it, that does not prove that the universe is a fraud. Probably earthly pleasures were never meant to satisfy it, but only to arouse it, to suggest the real thing. If that is so, I must take care, on the one hand, never to despise, or be unthankful for, these earthly blessings, and on the other, never to mistake them for the something else of which they are only a kind of copy, or echo, or mirage. I must keep alive in

24. Ibid., 129.
25. Ibid., 54.
26. Ibid., 144.
27. Ibid., 163.

myself the desire for my true country, which I shall not find till after death.[28]

Mundane liturgical theology recognizes the world's capacity to arouse. It is a theology of arousal, another way to speak of erotic theology. But our progress is a zigzag. Because we are in the image of God, we have a desire for God, and the icon will always seek its prototype; but because we are fallen, our desire regularly fastens upon inadequate objects. That is why it is so important to keep the desire alive. The cataphatic affirmation actually helps to bring about the apophatic negation. John says at one point, "I am afraid that the things the Landlord really intends for me may be utterly unlike the things he has taught me to desire," and Mr. History replies, "they will be very unlike the things you imagine. But you already know that the objects which your desire imagines are always inadequate to that desire. Until you have it you will not know what you wanted" (VIII.10). The two keys must work together. We imagine objects that correlate to the felt desire, and imagination is a golden key; but the objects we desire are always inadequate to the desire, and the silver key must unlock our fist so we are prepared to drop them. Once our desire has attained any finite object, we will know that this was not the true country for which we yearned. We must live from the paradoxical tension of neither spurning nor being satisfied with any earthly blessings. This is the antinomy that underlies mundane liturgical theology. We must neither curse this world nor can we be content with it. Liturgical asceticism both blesses the world and leaves the world, simultaneously. To find the treasure that will satisfy our desire, we must pick up every pebble with our right hand, and then drop it again with our left when we realize it is not the pearl of great price. And we must never tire of doing so, or we will forsake the journey of Affirmation that leads us to the gates of heaven.

When the apophatic and cataphatic integrate, emptiness is a fullness. That is why Lewis defined Romanticism as maintaining the original desire. Mr. Reason tells John, "consider also the Island. All

---

28. C.S. Lewis, *Mere Christianity* (San Francisco: Harper, 2009), 136–37.

that you know of it comes at last to this: that your first sight of it was yearning or wanting and that you have never ceased to want that first sight back, *as though you wanted a wanting*, as though the wanting were the having, and the having a wanting. What is the meaning of this hungry fruition and this emptiness which is the best filling?"[29] I submit that this is a description of our liturgical transaction with the world. We have; we are given gifts in abundance; we possess; and yet the having produces a wanting, if all is working properly. And the emptiness that results is the best filling. We are drawn beyond the world, but not because the world is bad. It is because the Island is not our final end and knowing our final end is a liturgical knowledge.

Recall Lewis describing earlier an experience of hunger that was better than fullness, and poverty that was better than wealth. Surely this is what he was trying to express in Narnia when the good mare Hwin meets Aslan for the first time, a scene that I consider to be the basis of liturgical asceticism. She trots up to the lion, trembling, and says: "Please, you are so beautiful. You may eat me if you like. I would sooner be eaten by you than fed by anyone else."[30] Lewis has another, and unexpected, name for it. This is "an unsatisfied desire which is itself more desirable than any other satisfaction. I call it Joy."[31] One cannot understand the spiritual effort toward self-annihilation unless one knows that joy waits at the end. The Orthodox ascetics loved to apophatically combine contrasting qualities, such as sober inebriation and illuminating darkness. Here is Lewis's offering to the list: satisfying insatiability. He discovered that we do not desire the object, we desire the desire. We do not desire the object, we desire God, and we only desire any object in so far as it awakens our desire for Him. The way of Affirmation and Negation work in tension with each other, like climbing up a shaft by bracing your feet against opposing walls. Lewis says we must pursue false

29. C. S. Lewis, *The Pilgrim's Regress*, 170.

30. C. S. Lewis, *The Horse and His Boy*, in *The Chronicles of Narnia*, complete set (New York: HarperCollins Publishers, 2001), 299.

31. C. S. Lewis, *Surprised by Joy: The Shape of My Early Life* (New York: Harcourt, Brace, Jovanovich, 1966), 17.

objects until their falsity appears, and then resolutely abandon them.[32] If a staircase is constructed for the purpose of ascending from earth to heaven, each step on it may be good, but evil results if we stop climbing and sit on a particular step, like squatters. Even Eden should not have satisfied Adam and Eve. If we confuse the image with the prototype, the ectype with the archetype, then we sin and nature is profaned. This is the wrong that we can commit against the cosmos; we can make it "groan in travail" (Romans 8:22). Every pleasure, says Lewis, should be "shafts of the glory as it strikes our sensibility," and should be made into a "channel of adoration."[33] Glory and adoration are liturgical words.

Let us turn, finally, to the insights of Coventry Patmore, because the Tempter has another trick to play, and Patmore is especially forearming us by bringing us full circle. The Greek word for *sin* means "to miss the mark," and although no thing in the world is sinful, anything in the world may be used sinfully and miss its mark. As I have put it elsewhere, the problem is not money, sex, or beer; the problem is avarice, lust, and gluttony.[34] Patmore suggests that Satan is happy to play either side of the equation. "When the Tempter can no longer persuade us to our destruction by representing *unclean things as clean*, he perpetually harasses us, and endeavors to delay our progress by representing *clean things as unclean*."[35] First he hardens our conscience to the point that we excuse our avarice, lust, and gluttony as clean. Then, if our conscience is pricked, his diabolical jujitsu represents money, sex, and beer as unclean. The first deception is to persuade us to take something we should not, and

32. C.S. Lewis, *The Pilgrim's Regress*, preface, 15.

33. C.S. Lewis, *Letters to Malcolm* (New York: Mariner Books, 2002), 89.

34. David Fagerberg, "On Liturgical Fasting," in *Logos: A Journal of Eastern Christian Studies*, 48 nos. 1–2 (2007): 83–104.

35. Coventry Patmore, *The Rod, the Root, and the Flower* (London: George Bell and Sons, 1895), 157; emphasis added. I have been fascinated by the promise of Patmore to my conversion to Catholicism ever since reading a toss-away line by Chesterton which said that in his own conversion to Catholicism he came to understand "what Coventry Patmore meant when he said calmly that it would have been quite as Catholic to decorate his mantelpiece with the Venus of Milo as with the Virgin." *The Catholic Church and Conversion* in *Collected Works of G.K. Chesterton*, Vol. III (San Francisco: Ignatius Press, 1990), 94.

the second deception is to persuade us not to take something we are permitted. The first is a cajoling whisper in the ear of the hedonist that stifles proper ethics, the second is a derisive whisper in the ear of the puritan that stifles innocent enjoyment. Patmore's prescription? "In the first stage of our advance we are purified by self-denial, and the second by denial, almost equally laborious, of the enemy's false charges."[36] Which is more difficult for us? Hard to say, and it may need to be answered on an individual basis because different individuals are more susceptible to one or the other. But everyone faces both fronts in one degree or another. Desert asceticism is required lest we receive the world in a disordered manner; but mundane asceticism is required lest we overreact and think clean things unclean, a good world evil, and lose our capacity for affirming its images. In the first stage we advance by self-denial, in the second stage we advance by righteousness and true knowledge of the world. This is liturgical knowledge of the mundane.

When we are freed from the enemy's false charges, then the world is returned to us, as Patmore describes in one of his most brilliant entries in *The Rod, the Root, and the Flower*:

> Plato's cave of shadows is the most profound and simple statement of the relation of the natural to the spiritual life ever made. Men stand with their backs to the Sun, and they take the shadows cast by it upon the walls of their cavern for realities. The shadows, even, of heavenly realities are so alluring as to provoke ardent desires, but they cannot satisfy us. They mock us with unattainable good, and our natural and legitimate passions and instincts, in the absence of their true and substantial satisfactions, break forth into frantic disorders. If we want fruition we must turn our backs on the shadows, and gaze on their realities in God.
>
> It may be added that, when we have done this, and are weary of the splendours and felicities of immediate reality, we may turn again, from time to time, to the shadows, which, having thus become intelligible, and being attributed by us to their true origin, are immeasurably more satisfying than they were before, and may be delighted in without blame. This is the "evening joy," the joy of

---

36. Ibid., 157.

contemplating God in His creatures, of which the theologians write; and this purified and intelligible joy in the shadow—which has now obtained a core of substance—is not only the hundred-fold "promise of this life also," but it is, as the Church teaches, a large part of the joy of the blest.[37]

Our liberation results in the world becoming at last the liturgical environment it was intended to be for man and woman. The silver key turns its back on the shadows, the monk in the desert gazes on the reality of all things as they exist in God, Mary chooses the more excellent way. But afterward the shadows finally become intelligible, satisfying, delightful. The apophatic makes the cataphatic possible. Having left the world, we may return to it. How can we say the Island is all bad when longing for the Island has brought us this far? The objects of the world are not false for being unclean; the objects of the world only become false when we ascribe to them a meaning under whose weight they crack. Good things have evil effects when we use them to foster self-love. They will break because no finite thing was meant to bear our infinite desire. Only the Infinite One can satisfy a desire that is infinite. This is the liturgical state: knowing the world the way the world was meant to be known.

Gregory of Nyssa described the Way of Negation by using the Song of Songs metaphor of the bride stripping off her garments to be re-dressed for the wedding. Gregory portrays it as a never-ending process for the soul, because the soul is to constantly stretch herself forth from glory to glory (Paul's phrase in Romans). The soul is, in a true sense, transformed into the divine because it truly participates in the Dove; and yet, at the same time, God remains constantly beyond and the soul must yet again go out of herself. At each stage, the soul has every reason to think she is completely naked, not knowing the possibility of a greater purity; she could not know the present stage except in light of the subsequent one. After divesting herself of all further clothing, she has become purer than she was before; and yet, Gregory says, she does not seem to have so much as removed her head covering. "Thus in comparison with her new-

37. Ibid., 68–69.

found purity, that very stripping of her tunic now becomes a kind of garment which those who find her must once again remove."[38] Well, this process is also true, in a mirror image, of the Way of Affirmation. This time the soul is putting on more garments, more images, more gifts. And at each stage, the soul has every reason to think it is completely full, not knowing the possibility of a greater affirmation. Only the subsequent stage makes the antecedent fully known. Thus Patmore concludes, "'Detachment' consists, not in casting aside all natural loves and goods, but in the possession of a love and a good so great that all others, though they may and do acquire increase through the presence of the greater love and good, which explains and justifies them, seem nothing in comparison."[39]

Here, then, is the ultimate paradox: we can be led by the world to God, but only if we disown the world. Apophatic and cataphatic work together, in tension. "All men are led to Heaven by their own loves; but these must first be sacrificed."[40] Three times in his short book Patmore returns to the story of Abraham's aborted exterior sacrifice and successful interior sacrifice in order to describe the sacrifice a man must make. Here is the first. "Like Abraham, he has to offer up his first-born, his dearest possession, his 'ruling love,' whatever it may be. He must actually lift the knife—not so much to prove his sincerity to God as to himself."[41] Here is the second: "The soul must have lifted the knife to slay its most precious possession, before she can discern good from evil."[42] Here is the third: "'God leads us by our own desires,' after we have once offered the sacrifice of them with full sincerity. The 'ruling love,' the best-beloved good, which we offer to slay, as Abraham did Isaac, that very good is given back to us glorified and made indeed the thing which we desired."[43] This is the everlasting paradox. The world can be given back to us glorified because we are no longer using it for personal vainglory;

38. Gregory of Nyssa, commentary on the Song of Songs, selection in Daniélou, *From Glory to Glory*, 264.

39. Patmore, *The Rod, the Root, and the Flower*, 31.

40. Ibid., 33.

41. Ibid., 71.

42. Ibid., 120.

43. Ibid., 197.

now used for the glory of God alone, it becomes a liturgical place of sacrament and sacrifice. Our loves can lead us to the Creator when they no longer lead us to ourselves. The fundamental choice of every rational being is between liturgical posture and idolatrous posture (this was a fundamental choice for the angels, too, one that Lucifer failed). We can raise our hands in true *orans* only if we can discipline our proclivity to twist all things egocentrically. Creation was intended as a theophanous window upon the Creator, but the Enemy's smoke and mirrors trick us. Once our sight is restored, and we can see again with the eye of the Dove, then we can see the world as it was meant to be seen. And then, Patmore says, "the Enemy, who can assault us only through the flesh, has had his weapon taken out of his hands."[44] Satan is disarmed totally when neither this body, nor the world of sensate objects for which it is designed, can obstruct God. Then our flesh is no longer a weapon for Satan but a tool for God's kingdom; the same is true of money, sex, and beer.

Gregory of Nyssa earlier reminded us that vice is to virtue as blindness is to sight: the former in each case is a deprivation of a natural operation. Therefore, the battle against the vices comes about by the edification (building up) of the virtues. To explain this, Patmore offers an allegorical interpretation of Joshua, who did not directly attack the city of Jericho but surrounded it with blasts of his trumpets until the walls fell of themselves, representing the fact that flesh or senses do not fall through fighting, but rather "can only be overcome by the proclamation of an immediate and greater sensible good, than that which it is called upon to abandon."[45] How will anyone get beyond the world if they are using objects in the world to draw themselves forward? Something transcendent is needed, and it must be injected under us as a new foundation that will lift us. These are the virtues supernaturally invigorated. Water poured into a glass of oil will sink to the base and fill the glass from the bottom upward until all the oil has run off. This is virtue fracking vice. Humility's expansion pressures out vainglory, charity's increase

44. Ibid., 57.
45. Ibid., 135.

squeezes out envy, meekness withstands the waves of anger until they subside, poverty drains avarice, and so on. "Some one [sic] has said, 'Great is his happiness and safety who has beaten all his enemies, but far greater his to whom they have become friends and allies.' Happy he who has conquered his passions, but far happier he whose servants and friends they have become. The reconciled passions are the '*sure* mercies of David.'"[46]

As Abraham received back Isaac after he offered him up, and as we receive back the world after we are ready to sacrifice our ruling love, so even our zeal and fervor are received back, anew, refreshed, invigorated after the corruptions have been corrected. Faculties restored to their upright position carry righteous passions instead of sinful ones. The enemy has had this weapon taken out of his hand, too: the passions no longer work like passions.

> In vulgar minds the idea of passion is inseparable from that of disorder; in them the advances of love, or anger, or any other strong energy towards its end, is like the rush of a savage horde, with war-whoops, tom-toms, and confused tumult; and the great decorum of a passion, which keeps, and is immensely increased in force by, the discipline of God's order, looks to them like weakness and coldness. Hence the passions, which are the measure of man's capacity for virtues, are regarded by the pious vulgar as being of the nature of vice; and, indeed, in them they are so; for virtues are nothing but ordered passions, and vices nothing but passions in disorder.[47]

Thus, Patmore concludes, "Sanctity is not the negation of passion but its order."[48] Money, sex, and beer, bodies and appetites, carnal pleasures and social interactions, human affections and faraway Islands can again exercise their strong energy, like steeds under the reins of the divine charioteer. Earthly goods can arouse our appetite for heavenly goods so long as we do not fixate on them. Patmore thought that the Catholic Church had been nearly killed by the

---

46. Ibid., 166.
47. Ibid., 146.
48. Ibid., 40.

infection of a puritanism that stemmed from the Reformation, and, as a result, conjugal love was branded with a charge of impurity, studiously ignored, and sometimes positively condemned as carnal.[49] But the Incarnation was a sanctification of our bodies as well as our souls, and the supernatural settles, as a dewfall, upon every natural thing. "Nature fulfilled by grace is not less natural, but is supernaturally natural."[50]

Williams said Patmore expressed this by Eucharistic example when he wrote, "The Blessed Sacrament is first of all a symbol of the beloved; afterwards the beloved is a symbol of the Blessed Sacrament." Upon that remark Williams pronounced, "Such a pregnant saying has conceived within it the whole of Romantic Theology."[51] If I concur, I do not intend to do so cheaply. It denigrates the cross to suggest that our salvation is nothing but an adjustment of an intellectual perception. Our salvation has cost two deaths, after all, Christ's and ours. But Williams is not offering us a cheap version of Romantic Theology. He rests the Way of Affirmation not upon our transcendental tickles, but instead squarely upon the doctrine of the Incarnation: "The maxim of this way is in the creed of Saint Athanasius: 'not by conversion of the Godhead into flesh, but by taking of the Manhood into God.'"[52] By the Incarnation, Christ stooped down in order to put his shoulder under the human race and lift us up. (The footing he needed to accomplish this was in Hades, and when he pushed toward heaven again its gates shattered.) From Athanasius's assertion that the Word made himself a bearer of the flesh in order that human beings might become bearers of the spirit, we may conclude that every human energy is capable of bearing

---

49. Ibid., 201.

50. Ibid., 7.

51. Williams, *Outlines of Romantic Theology*, 36. In *The Figure of Beatrice* Williams refers to Patmore as someone who drew attention to the Eucharistic relevance of the procession and appearance of Beatrice, saying again that this is the heart of Romantic Theology. "It is sufficient here to render Patmore's maxim in *The Rod, the Root and Flower*: 'the Holy Eucharist, in the beginning, is desired because it resembles the lower but still "great" sacrament of human affection; afterwards the lower sacrament is explained and glorified by its resemblance to the higher'" (188).

52. Williams, *The Figure of Beatrice*, 9.

transfigured significance. About the Eucharist, Williams says "the distance between an ordinary meal and that nourishment which is communicated in the Eucharist should lessen, as it were, until perhaps to the devout soul every meal is an actual Eucharist in the theological sense."[53] About marriage, Patmore says, "Lovers are nothing else than Priest and Priestess to each other of the Divine Manhood and the Divine Womanhood which are in God."[54] About the transmission of life through sexual intercourse in marriage, Pius XI says it makes "parents the ministers, as it were, of the Divine Omnipotence."[55] Now we find glimpses of heaven on earth, traces of agape in Romantic Theology. About his own falling in romantic love with his wife Joy, Lewis said, "It is nice to have arrived at all of this by something which began in Agape, proceeded to Philia, then became Pity, and only after that, Eros. As if the highest of these, Agape, had successfully undergone the sweet humiliation of an incarnation."[56]

The world can only be sacramental for fallen man and woman if Christ makes it so. Fallen man and woman can only participate in the world's sacramentality if they are first delivered from sin by the power of grace that flows from Christ's pierced side to pool up in the Church's sacraments. Mundane liturgical theology does not suppose we can do without ecclesial sacraments (this heresy has reared its head numerous times in the history of the Church, and I mean to avoid it here), but if we acknowledge the ascetical cost of conversion then we will find that the cultic liturgy animates our lived liturgy, and the latter is what mundane liturgical theology wishes to describe. Liturgy will involve doing the world the way the world was meant to be done, and then

> it will be as if all the infinite forms which lie hidden and possible to the sculptor in a block of marble should exist and be distinctly

53. Williams, *Outlines of Romantic Theology*, 9.

54. Patmore, *The Rod, the Root, and the Flower*, 113.

55. Pius XI, *Casti Connubii*, Encyclical on Christian Marriage (31 December 1930), ¶80.

56. Letter by Lewis to Dom Bede Griffiths on 24 September 1957, quoted by Walter Hooper in *C. S. Lewis: A Complete Guide to His Life and Works* (New York: HarperSanFrancisco, 1966), 83.

discerned at one and the same moment. Hence it is that, in the process of sanctification, each soul is safely led by her own desires, which God gives her back glorified directly she has made a sincere sacrifice of them. He says, not only "Let the Heavens rejoice," but, "Philistia be glad of me."[57]

This rejoicing in Philistia is mundane liturgy.

57. Patmore, *The Rod, the Root, and the Flower*, 178.

2

The Ear of the Dove

❧

C. S. Lewis remarked that "the joys of Heaven are, for most of us in our present condition, 'an acquired taste.'"[1] We must be prepared for beatitude, and, oddly enough, sometimes against our will. I do not mean without our will, but that our will must be overturned for us to be returned to God. Lewis's friend, Dorothy Sayers, identifies what conversion is required for beatitude: "When we sin, we alienate ourselves from God; and if we are ever to be happy in His presence again, it is something in us that has to be altered—not anything in Him."[2] Without this new mind (*metanoia*, conversion), we will never feel at home with God. In fact, being in his presence will be hellish instead of heavenly. Therefore, to accomplish his great plan of salvation (the *mysterium magnum* of which Paul speaks in Ephesians 5) God must get under our skin and alter our tastes, and the Holy Spirit is just the person for the job. An eschatological attraction exerts its force when awakened by the Dove.

Rabbi Baal Shem Tov was founder of the Hasidic movement in Judaism and asked once why its members swayed during prayer, and might burst into song and dance at the slightest provocation. He responded with a story about a musician who played on a street corner. Those who stopped to listen were enthralled by the music, and before long were moving to its rhythm. But a deaf man walking by wondered if they had all gone mad. The Rabbi was saying that Hasidic mystics could hear the melody that issues forth from every creature in God's creation.

1. C. S. Lewis, *The Problem of Pain* (New York: Macmillan, 1962), 61.
2. Dorothy Sayers, "The Meaning of Heaven and Hell," in *Introductory Papers on Dante* (New York: Harper and Brothers, 1954), 80.

There is another melody interwoven into the harmony of the spheres, and this one issues forth from heaven. It is an eschatological melody to which the Holy Spirit attunes us. Baptism will wash out our ears and make them attentive again to the melody issuing forth from creatures in God's creation, to the still, small voice that Elijah once heard, and now, most of all, to the distant strains of glory already pressing from the eschaton into our present world. While in the world, Christians live with the light of glory in their eyes, with the perfume of Christ in their nostrils, with the bread of immortality in their mouth, and they are given the ear of the Dove to hear the eschatological melody in their ears.

Here is a different image for the eschaton's irruption into history. River estuaries are places where a freshwater river meets a saltwater sea, and it results in a certain turbulence. Sea water noses into the estuary beneath the outflowing river water, pushing its way upstream along the bottom. This continual bottom flow provides a ventilation system, drawing in new oceanic water and expelling brackish water, without which the waters would become stagnant, pollution would accumulate, and oxygen would be depleted. But when this flushing process is present, an incredible ecological productivity is created by the oxygen being continually resupplied from the ocean, leading to some of the highest growths of microscopic plants in any marine environment, which in turn serve as a base for a variety of food webs. I propose that Christians live in an eschatological estuary. Actually, all human beings live under this ecology, not only Christians, because all humanity is being carried along the river of history toward the Divine Sea, but I single out the Church now because Christians are the people who are aware of what is causing the turbulence. Not only aware of it, they are enlisted as its agents. The sacramental eddy fuels a redemptive ecosystem of which Christians are a product.

God is already nosing his way into our lives, creating our very Christian identity. Here are the words on the walls of the Lateran baptistery, possibly written by Pope Leo the Great:

Here is born in Spirit-soaked fertility
a brood destined for another City,

begotten by God's blowing
and borne upon this torrent
by the Church their virgin mother. . . .
This spring is life that floods the world,
the wounds of Christ its awesome source.
Sinner sink beneath this sacred surf
that swallows age and spits up youth.
Sinner here scour sin away down to innocence. . . .
Sinner shudder not at sin's kind and number,
for those born here are holy.[3]

It is a tumultuous surf because eschatology is mainly about judgment, and judgment is the revelation of things as they really are. One day that judgment will be apocalyptic (all masks ripped off), but it has already begun in the liturgy and overshadows our lives.

God has infiltrated every human soul, and therefore every human culture has had a theory to explain the instability they perceive within. Some philosophers thought this was a Manichaean estuary. That is, they thought that the commotion we feel is caused by a conflict between matter and spirit. Philosophers have harbored the suspicion from Plato onward that the volatility in our mundane lives comes from the conflict between body and soul. They were misled by assuming the conflict was between the corporeal and the incorporeal, but they did at least notice a truth even in being wrong. (Our modern materialists are far more wrong when they say there is no soul, therefore there is no conflict, therefore we can make ourselves at home in the material without seeking anything loftier. Plato was wrong, but he was more right than our modern philosophers are.) But Christians believe that the tumult we feel is not caused by a conflict between matter and spirit; it is caused by the arrival of the new age in the old fallen one. This is an eschatological estuary, not a Gnostic one. Christian theology inherited from Israel the revelation that the created world is good: bodies are good, matter is good, souls in material bodies is a good state—so good, indeed, that a disembodied soul is an imperfection still waiting for the resurrection of its

---

3. Aidan Kavanagh's translation, *The Shape of Baptism* (New York: Pueblo Press, 1978), 49.

body. The whirlpool we feel below our feet is not from the strain of a soul living in a body, it is from the turbulence of a new age meeting the current age, the encroachment of the Divine Sea under us, even though we still swim in the flow of history. Our uneasiness does not derive from the fact that the world is not good, it derives from the fact that the world is not final. Christian asceticism does not say the body fell, it says that the whole man fell, but the result is that the body does not serve the spirit as it should.

The fall was the forfeiture of our liturgical career. Man and woman were created as royal priests to rule over creation and under God in the cosmic hierarchy. By failing to stand under God, their dominion went awry; failing to rule over creation, their priesthood went unfulfilled. We are their children. Louis Bouyer describes what the cosmic hierarchy should have been when he pictures it as a golden ladder of being, down which flows God's creative love and up which flows creation's eucharistic response:

> Across this continuous chain of creation, in which the triune fellowship of the divine persons has, as it were, extended and propagated itself, moves the ebb and flow of the creating Agape and of the created eucharistia.... Thus this immense choir of which we have spoken, basing ourselves on the Fathers, finally seems like an infinitely generous heart, beating with an unceasing diastole and systole, first diffusing the divine glory in paternal love, then continually gathering it up again to its immutable source in filial love.[4]

The ladder is composed of everything that goes forth from the hand of the Uncreated, down to the last actual occasion (Whitehead). The angels have their place in this hierarchy, since it includes heavenly being. The angelic Prince of this World, the morning star, the shining one, Lucifer, was supposed to diffuse the light of God upon the earth, and gather up earth's praise to God Almighty. But the Prince of Light became the Prince of Darkness. The fall of both angel and man is idolatry, and Lucifer became Satan when he idolatrously

---

4. Louis Bouyer, *The Meaning of the Monastic Life* (London: Burns & Oates, 1955), 28–29.

reserved earth's glory to himself and would not hand it over to God. He broke rank—he broke hierarchy. He sprained creation. The result was evil.

This accounts for a mystery. The created world is not evil, but there is evil in this world. This accounts for the combination of the negation and affirmation of images. Since Augustine, theologians have been clear that evil is the absence of a good, as darkness is the absence of light, and not vice versa. But Thomas adds to what he inherits, as he so often does. He says that not all cases of a good's absence are evil; only certain cases. For example, mere negation does not display the character of evil, otherwise nonexisting would be evil. But it is not evil that something does not exist. And by way of a second example, a thing is not evil for not possessing a goodness that properly belongs to another being. It is not evil that a bird cannot speak and I cannot fly, but it would be evil if flight was absent in the bird and speech was absent in me. We must therefore add a further qualification to the definition of evil: evil is the absence of a *perfection* that a being *ought* to have. All natures serve a purpose, and off the nature we can read the being's telos. Evil is diversion from the good which is consonant with the teleological end for which the nature of that particular being was made. Evil is the absence of the perfection toward which something ought to tend. Evil is failing to arrive at one's final home.

We are thus led to this teleological question: What is a perfect man or woman? And I reply, "a liturgist."

Surely this requires a thicker notion of liturgy than the term normally commands. We are not talking about temple etiquette or rubrical rulings. Too often when we think about liturgy we think only about the tip of it that we can see. The tip of the liturgical iceberg is the public ceremony done in ritualized form, but it is actually connected to a massive reality below the waterline. Of course, the liturgy has a visible ceremonial face, but this is not all it is: the water in the well that we can reach by the rope of our ritual bucket is only a part of the whole aquifer. To fully comprehend the ritual liturgy we must appreciate the saving economy that it epiphanizes, and eschatology can thicken our understanding of liturgy. The liturgy celebrates the Paschal mystery, and that mystery stands at the center of a timeline that stretches between the protological alpha and the eschatological omega. Everything leads up to it, and everything flows out of it. By its anamnetic and epicletic link to the Paschal mystery, liturgy brings heavenly activity to earth. Thus Pius XII's definition of liturgy:

> The sacred liturgy is, consequently, the public worship which our Redeemer as Head of the Church renders to the Father, as well as the worship which the community of the faithful renders to its Founder, and through Him to the heavenly Father. It is, in short, the worship rendered by the Mystical Body of Christ in the entirety of its Head and members. (*Mediator Dei* ¶20)

The liturgy is our inclusion, made possible by the Dove, in a relationship between the Son and the Father: (i) The Son worships the Father; (ii) the Church worships the Son, her founder; (iii) and through the Son, together with the Son, the Church worships the Father. All this occurs by the power of the Holy Spirit who is ushering creation into its own home: a redeemed, eschatological, spiritual existence. When mother Church said in the second Vatican Council that she "earnestly desires that all the faithful should be led to that full, conscious, and active participation in liturgical celebrations,"[5] she was not speaking about our right to ritual, she was speaking about our title to spiritual life. This kind of participation is the Christian's right and duty by reason of their baptism, and confirms their eschatological identity as a chosen race, a royal priesthood, a holy nation, a people of the Dove. The sort of nature that men and women were given at their creation is a nature designed for committing liturgy. A perfect human being is a liturgist; that is their place in the hierarchical ladder.

Hierarchy exists for the purpose of agape descending creatively, and glorification ascending eucharistically: hierarchy is a liturgical thoroughfare. And the reason for every being in the hierarchy—both heavenly and earthly—is to pass love from Creator to creation, and glory from creation to Creator. This passage of love is a particular mission of the Holy Spirit. Wherein lies sin? In willful idolatry.

---

5. *Sacrosanctum Concilium*, ¶14.

When Lucifer willed to take glory to himself, he was rebelling against his liturgical status. Sin is idolatrous from the start: it is failure to give right adoration, to rightly glorify, to worship righteously. Satan fell with such force that he bent creation and filled it with other nonhierarchical powers, i.e., powers that also broke hierarchy. These are the rulers of the present darkness of which the New Testament epistles speak, powers against whom we find ourselves helpless because "our struggle is not with flesh and blood but with the principalities, with the powers, with the world rulers of this present darkness, with evil spirits in the heavens" (Ephesians 6:12). Our father and mother were given natures that capacitated them for a role in the liturgical hierarchy, therefore Gregory of Nyssa called them a "small universe." Man and woman are microcosmic beings ("small houses"—*micro cosmos*) who had, in themselves, everything that God had created, material and spiritual, so they could restore the cosmic diastole and systole, like new arteries growing to bypass blocked ones. But, alas, Satan dislocated them, too. Our father and mother were all too easily seduced into his rebellion, and, having willfully joined him, their children are helpless before the spiritual wickedness of which the New Testament epistle speaks. They went deaf.

The New Testament uses the term *arche* to speak of these powers and principalities, rulers which, although illegitimate, are powerful enough to hold us captive. Our wrestling is in vain if done out of our own strength. That is why all the soteriological vocabulary in Christianity must be followed by the word "from." We say saved, delivered, redeemed, rescued—*from* what? Saved and rescued from what? Our soteriology is weakened in exactly the same degree that a theology of Satan is ignored. Eschatology is the story of Satan's ultimate defeat. Lose consciousness of the devil, and you lose the fullness of an understanding of redemption. Lose consciousness of a battle, and redemption is transmuted into personal psychotherapy. Eschatology is the concluding chapter to the history of a single, unceasing battle waged between the woman and the serpent, begun in Genesis, but whose end is foreseen by John from the island of Patmos. If we were to lose hope for an eschatological victory over Satan, our Christian vocabulary of redemption would be hollowed out, and our liturgical celebration would become the equivalent of personal, spiritual narcissism.

But the tide has turned. With the ear of the Dove we can hear the tones of the perichoresis. The eschatological current has begun nosing its way upstream, underneath the flow of history, and pools up in baptismal fonts everywhere. Christianity is the next world itself, present now in a mystery. In this heavy water, Christians are baptized into the priesthood of Christ in order to have their cosmic priesthood restored. The baptized are returned to Adam and Eve's liturgical place, vacant since their expulsion from Eden. The early Church understood the baptistery as the gate to paradise, formerly guarded by an angel with a fiery sword but now reopened by the cross and resurrection of Jesus. The cross is the key to the lock on the gate. This is only possible because among all the other principalities in the world, a different *arche* is offered us: a *hierus-arche*, a priestly power. Planted at the center point of sin, law, wrath, death, and the devil, as if standing in the middle of Hades, hung upon a cross just outside the walls of the city Jerusalem that is the navel of the world, is the action of the High Priest, whose sacrifice penetrates heaven. The radiation from the empty tomb causes our deification, and, if faith is receptive, places us under a different *arche* than the rebellious ones strangling the world. We are grafted into Christ's *hierus-arche*, Christ's priestly hierarchy. His mystical body is animated by the spiritual Dove. The Head shares with his Body the power to make that priestly sacrifice and serve the redemption of the world.

We take on the imprint of the altar of the Mass in order to ourselves become the sacrificial city of God in our bodies, in the midst of the irreligious city of man. There we practice our mundane liturgy. We become a priestly people, our life becomes sacrificial, and we go about our business hardly noticed except that we are stunningly normal as we do the world the way the world was meant to be done. "The ascetic is simply a stunningly normal person," says Kavanagh, "who stands in constant witness to the normality of Christian *orthodoxia* in a world flawed into abnormality by human choice."[6] This seems to be the very meaning that Dionysius had in mind when he coined the word hierarchy as a neologism:

In my opinion, a hierarchy is a sacred order, a state of understanding and an activity approximating as closely as possible to the divine. The goal of a hierarchy, then, is to enable beings to be as like as possible to God and to be one with him. A hierarchy has God as its leader of all understanding and action. It is forever looking directly at the comeliness of God. . . . Hierarchy causes its members to be images of God in all respects, to be clear and spotless mirrors reflecting the glow of primordial light and indeed of God himself. It ensures that when its members have received this full and divine splendor they can then pass on this light generously and in accordance with God's will to beings further down the scale.[7]

Yves Congar says hierarchy means "having a sacred power" and defines it as "spiritual powers tending to salvation."[8] Therefore, when asked whether the Church is hierarchical, the correct answer is "I hope so." Flannery O'Connor famously said that if the Eucharist is only a symbol, then to hell with it; also, if the Church is only the Jesus club, then to hell with it. We need a hierarchical institution with a spiritual power tending to salvation.

The second Adam has done what the first Adam failed to do. Christ did the world the way the world was meant to be done, and this second Adam is a new Liturgist, who invites our participation as his liturgical apprentices. Though the cost of doing the world righteously was the cross, the second Adam persisted in his worship of the Father, and at the end invested us with his liturgy. What is the true Christian spirit (*Sacrosanctum Concilium* 14) that we are to derive from the liturgy? The one found in Christ, the one found in Christ's hypostatic union. This is where a human will was finally fully conformed to the will of God—something intended for the first Adam, but not accomplished. The first Adam did not have

6. Aidan Kavanagh, *On Liturgical Theology*, 161.

7. Dionysius, *The Celestial Hierarchy*, ch. 3. This translation from *Pseudo-Dionysius, the Complete Works*, translation by Colm Luibheid, The Classics of Western Spirituality (New York: Paulist Press, 1987), 153–54.

8. Yves Congar, *Lay People in the Church* (Westminster: The Newman Press, 1965), 353.

equality with God, but grasped at it; the second Adam did have equality with God, but emptied himself into only one desire: to obey the Father, to love the Father, to be near the Father. George MacDonald (the Scottish preacher in whom C.S. Lewis said he could "smell holiness") puts it this way:

> His whole thought, his whole delight, was in the thought, in the will, in the being of his Father. The joy of the Lord's life, that which made it life to him, was the Father; of him he was always thinking, to him he was always turning. I suppose most men have some thought of pleasure or satisfaction or strength to which they turn when action pauses, life becomes for a moment still, and the wheel sleeps on its own swiftness: with Jesus it needed no pause of action, no rush of renewed consciousness, to send him home; his thought was ever and always his Father. To its home in the heart of the Father his heart ever turned. That was his treasure-house, the jewel of his mind, the mystery of his gladness, claiming all degrees and shades of delight, from peace and calmest content to ecstasy. His life was hid in God.[9]

In other words, Jesus's life was eschatological. The Dove which alit on him at the Jordan baptism never left him, and when we are baptized into him the Dove comes along, too. The Second Adam has given that Spirit to the Second Eve (the Church), also brought into the world by virgin birth—i.e., a birth brought about by the Spirit and not by human agency. The Church is taken from the side of Jesus as he slept in death on the cross, as the first Eve was taken from the side of the first Adam during his deep sleep. By obedience, the second Eve unties the knot of disobedience into which the first Eve had tied herself. This obedience restores the liturgical hierarchy. This obedience gives spiritual birth to a new race growing toward perfection.

The reason for coupling liturgy and eschatology is so that the latter can serve as a thickening agent upon our understanding of the former. Doing the world liturgically, as it was meant to be done, proves difficult to sinners. A man with a crooked leg cannot walk

---

9. George MacDonald, *Unspoken Sermons, First, Second and Third Series* (Whitehorn, CA: Johannsen, 1999), 171.

straight, and we of crooked hearts cannot walk through the world upright. The eschatological vision is a forecast of the day when everything within creation becomes righteous; it is a forecast of our final home to which we are being lifted up. But already, in hope, we hear the choirs of the Book of Revelation and join them in offering the holy oblation in peace. All liturgies (hours, year, sacraments, the Mass) should shine with this quality of eschatological victory. Human worship of God is a good thing, but the Christian liturgy is not one of Adam's religions; the eschatological liturgy is not a species in the genus of natural religion. The Christian liturgy is the cult of the new Adam, the sacrificial adoration of the Son to the Father, perpetuated in Christians by the Holy Spirit. Schmemann said that the loss of this eschatological dimension has caused a metamorphosis of our liturgical consciousness. We cock our heads, but we do not hear properly:

> The Church is not a natural community which is "sanctified" through the cult. In its essence the Church is the presence, the actualization in this world of the "world to come," in this *aeon*—of the kingdom. And the mode of this presence, of this actualization of the new life, the new *aeon*, is precisely the *leitourgia*. It is only within this eschatological dimension of the Church that one can understand the nature of the liturgy: to actualize and realize the identity of the *ecclesia* with the new *aeon*, of the "age to come."[10]

Satan's labor is to lie about this world and God's place in it, and the liturgical form of resistance to his lie is exorcism. We tend to understand exorcism as "casting out," as though Satan were resident in an object, like a cork stuck in a bottle neck. This is an understandable impression, since an obstruction must be removed. But the far more adequate definition of exorcism is "reclaiming something for its original purpose." Satan's lie must be exposed, true, and we must cast him behind us, but the real aim of exorcism is to reclaim something that has belonged to God from the beginning. Christ comes to

---

10. Alexander Schmemann, "Theology and Liturgical Tradition," in *Liturgy and Tradition: Theological Reflections of Alexander Schmemann*, ed. Thomas Fisch (Crestwood, NY: St. Vladimir's Seminary Press, 1990), 16.

do so. The catechumens of the early Church underwent frequent exorcisms in their order of initiation because the entire catechumenate existed precisely for the purpose of reclaiming a particular human being for Christ. The believer underwent a *transitus* from death to life, from darkness to light, from sin to righteousness, from serpent to Dove, from Satan's household to Christ's household. It was as if the rope holding them captive was so thick that it could not be cut with one stroke, but at each daily exorcism a few more binding threads were cut until the neophyte was totally freed at the night of baptism. The exorcisms before baptism were, in that way, a counterpoise to the mark made on the neophyte's forehead after their washing. The Latin tradition has called it a character; the Greek-speaking mystagogues called it a *sphragis*, a word describing a mark of ownership and belonging. A *sphragis* was tattooed upon soldiers to mark their identity in the army, and a *sphragis* was branded into the flesh of the sheep and the slave to indicate their owner. But the character worked in both directions: the shepherd not only owned the sheep, the shepherd was also obliged to protect his sheep. The baptized Christian, who had belonged to the household of Satan, now belonged to the household of Christ and was under his protection. The sign of the cross is like the *sphragis* of Cain, placed upon him for protection, lest anyone (Satan, for example) should try to kill him on sight (Genesis 4:15). Making the sign of the cross is an apotropaic act, too.

The pre-baptismal exorcisms annulled the claims Satan had falsely filed, and they simultaneously reclaimed not only the individual, but more. In exorcising and reclaiming the catechumen, the Church was also exorcising and reclaiming the City of Man in which he lived. Josef Jungmann describes what it meant when the one being baptized said "I renounce thee, Satan, and all your works, and all your pomp, and all your service." He describes the Christian renunciation by explaining the origin of the word "pomp":

A *pompa* was, in the culture of antiquity, a festive procession, a triumphal procession, a marching around at some god's feast, at which all idols were carried along. The devil is, as it were, constantly conducting such a triumphal procession in the world; all who serve the devil and live in sin are running along in this procession. But in baptism the candidate drops out of this procession, leaves the devil's camp, and enters into the camp of Christ's Army.[11]

Satan has tried to fence off the world from God by this diabolical circumambulation. If he succeeds, the sons of Adam and daughters of Eve will never be at home in this world, and there will be no affirmation of its mundane images. In an old (1873) but still valuable book, Fustel de Coulanges describes the way the city of Rome was founded according to the ancient sources. A city did not accumulate by the slow increase of population and houses, it was founded all at once, entirely in a day, by plowing a trench around the central worship hearth, a trench that established the perimeter of the city. Upon this boundary the walls of the city would be built up.[12] All of Satan's claims to custody are bogus, since he is duplicitous and a liar, and he has no city of his own, so he walks round God's creation in his pseudo-triumphant procession attempting to claim possession of something he was not given. But Christ has broken the *pompa* by symbolical reunion. The Incarnation broke through Satan's *pompa* and reclaimed the whole world for liturgical purpose: and with that the eschaton has dawned. All matter, all time, all natural being and all human artifacts are now available for symbolic/sacramental purpose. The material world can once again mediate the dialogue between God and man because we have been given ears to hear it, and so the material world is finally at peace. It can be used the way it was meant to be used: this is what the liturgical symbolism in the Book of Revelation is communicating.

In the rites of initiation the ears are signed with the cross that the catechumen may hear the voice of the Lord; in the earlier form the priest touched the right and left ear and said "Ephphetha, that is, be opened." It has an exorcistic flavor because the demons trouble us

---

11. Josef Jungmann, *The Early Liturgy to the Time of Gregory the Great* (Notre Dame: University of Notre Dame Press, 1977), 80.

12. Fustel de Coulanges, *The Ancient City: A Classic Study of the Religious and Civil Institutions of Ancient Greece and Rome* (New York: Doubleday Anchor Books, 1956), 134–37.

by stopping up our ears, preventing us from hearing, and we are now being given new ears. Let him who has them, hear.

In the current prayers of exorcism in the Christian Initiation of Adults, the catechumen bows or kneels before the celebrant who, with hands outstretched over them, has a number of prayers to choose from. He may ask the God of power, who promised the Holy Spirit, to protect the catechumens from the spirit of evil so that they may become the temple of God's Holy Spirit; he may ask the God who cuts away corruption to remove from his servants all unbelief and hesitation in faith, because God has called them to be holy and sinless in his sight; he may ask the God who created man and woman in his image and likeness to free his servants from the evil and tyranny of the enemy, and receive them into his kingdom so they may become members of his Church; he may ask the Lord Jesus, who turned his disciples from the paths of sin, to protect these servants from the spirit of greed, lust, and pride; he may ask the Creator and Savior of all to probe their hearts and complete the plan of love in them; he may ask God, who knows the secrets of our hearts, to look kindly on the efforts of these servants and strengthen them, and accept their repentance; he may ask Jesus, whose name alone has the power to save, to free them from the snares and malice of Satan; he may ask the Lord Jesus to not let their lives be tied to earthly troubles, estranged from the hope of his promises; he may ask Jesus, who calmed the storms, and freed the possessed, and called Matthew the tax collector, to hold in check the power of the evil one, and heal the wounds of sin; he may ask the God of infinite wisdom to probe their hearts and purify them so they may be freed from all deception; or he may ask the Creator and Redeemer to purify their hearts, bring them to fulfillment, and let them drink the waters of salvation. There are eleven prayers of exorcism. Their wording describes the effects of an exorcism. The rubrics explaining the use of this rite to the universal Church mention "regions where false worship is widespread," places where spiritual powers are worshiped or people use magical arts, but, really, can we imagine any region where false worship is not widespread? The purpose of the exorcism is to reclaim this person as cosmic priest, and the world in which he lives as a liturgical environs.

This is possible because Jesus takes sin upon himself, drawing out the poison of the serpent bite. He applies his cross as a poultice to our wound. At one Good Friday procession in which the congregation advanced to reverence the cross, I saw the priest afterward carry the wooden cross to the side pews, to the elderly in wheelchairs and the infirmed with their walkers. At first glance, it seemed almost cruel: had they not suffered enough, and now the priest was bringing the tree of suffering for them to embrace? But I had it backward. He was bringing the tree of victory to them, the throne which Christ still keeps precisely so that he may take our suffering upon himself. They did not kiss the cross in order to take Christ's suffering upon themselves, they kissed it in order to lay their suffering upon him. Isaac of Nineveh described the effects of grace by saying that when a drop of black ink is spilled on a white linen, amazingly the ink is turned white instead of the linen being stained black. It was the same for the woman with a hemorrhage, who did not pollute Christ with her touch, but was herself healed by the touch she dared. And it was the same here for these congregants, who were not taking on more suffering, rather Christ was taking on theirs. It was an action in which Christ was trained by his Jewish heritage. In a Holocaust novel, Andre Schwarz-Bart composes a conversation between a young Jewish boy and an elderly Jewish tailor who has lost his faith in the existence of God. "That night on his mattress set directly on the floor Benjamin tried to picture all things as Mr. Goldfaden must see them. Bit by bit he arrived at the terrifying conclusion that if God did not exist, Zemyock [their town] was only an absurd fragment of the universe. But then, he wondered, where does all the suffering go?"[13]

How is the isolating ditch of alienation filled in? How was Satan bound when Christ entered this world to steal us from the strong man? How was Hades forced to disgorge its inhabitants? (Divine syrup of ipecac must also have flowed with the blood and water from his pierced side.) The cross is a tree of victory, and therefore

13. Andre Schwartz-Bart, *The Last of the Just* (New York: Atheneum House, 1960), 77.

an eschatological sign. Drawing on studies by Erik Peterson, Ratzinger concludes that this was how the early Church saw the cross, but he worries that succeeding generations may have lost their vision. The cross on the east wall of Christian meeting-houses was first "seen as a sign of the returning Christ; later it became more and more a reminder of the Lord's historical Passion, and finally the eschatological idea disappeared almost entirely from the image of the cross."[14] Eschatology's major symbol of victory over Satan is a warp that must be woven into every liturgical woof, or else the liturgy is just whistling past the graveyard. Without the sacramental presence of the eschatological victory, the liturgy becomes the Jesus club whispering comforting platitudes to itself while in a holding pattern over death.

Thomas insisted on three dimensions to every sacrament: past, present, and future. All sacraments are tricloptic: they commemorate the passion of Christ, bring about our justification and increase charity, and point us to our heavenly beatitude. But maybe we would be better off using other terms, because the words "past, present, and future" are all on the same timeline. When we use these words, accident of language tempts us to refer to the eschatological *aeon* as a future portion of this *aeon*, as if it's the next chapter of the same book. We are subtly influenced by Hegel's metanarrative that says history progresses, and thus misinterpret eschatology as some sort of progression to a future point of a line on which we already stand. In that case, where is the abrupt, kairotic, perpendicular line of conversion? The *aeon* that is actualized liturgically is not just the future, it is eternity. The *aeon* that is actualized liturgically is a divine act of God already nosing its way upstream into every baptized believer's life. So rather than "past, present, and future" let us rather say that all sacraments are *historical, sacramental,* and *eschatological.* Omitting any one of these does great injustice to any sacrament. Omit the historical, and the sacrament turns into a mythology without actual accomplishment; omit the sacramental, and liturgy becomes mere instruction, a sign that is not efficacious;

14. Joseph Ratzinger, *The Feast of Faith* (San Francisco: Ignatius Press, 1986), 141.

omit the eschatological, and liturgy is no longer a ground for our hope. The three relate perichoretically.

Zeno's paradox said that if we only go halfway to a boundary we will never cross that border because the distance to it can always be divided in half. If I go always, but only, halfway to the door's threshold we can move ever closer (10 feet, 5, 2.5, 1.25, to infinity) but never get out of the room. We must have a target on the other side of the boundary. The mountain climber must tether his hook to something higher than the rock face if he is to transcend the peak. If our borderline is the last point of the temporal line on which we already stand, the human race will get forever nearer to death but never transcend this *aeon*. And any citizen of this temporal line, no matter how morally inspired or philosophically wise, can only bring me by halves to a threshold I will never cross. Only Christ can bring us far enough because his resurrection offers the new *aeon* as our teleological point. He has made it possible to transcend the boundary line of history, to eternity. His *hodie* (hour) transcends the historical timeline which it irrupted. Without his eschatological act, we will never get beyond death, we will only creep toward it infinitely.

The Church Fathers spoke about the final conquering of cyclical time as the eighth day. It is a conclusion of history precisely because it is beyond history, and therefore brings history to closure. Sunday does not celebrate the Sabbath rest that exists at the end part of the history we are in; Sunday celebrates an eternal eighth day irrupting from beyond history. And we can step into that eighth day even now. It is one thing to rest in the Lord while being in the midst of time, symbolized by the Sabbath; it is another thing to go beyond all time and rest in the Maker of time, symbolized by the eighth day. Sunday, the premier liturgical day, preserves the eschatological expectation among Christians, and becomes a symbol of the passage which is the Church. The eighth-day *kairos* existence is expressed and manifested as cult, says Schmemann:

> She is the passage of the "old" into the "new"—yet what is being redeemed, renewed and transfigured through her is not the "Church," but the old life itself, the old Adam and the whole of creation. And she is this "passage" precisely because as institution she

is "bone of the bones and flesh of the flesh" of this world. . . . She is indeed instituted for the world and not as a separate "religious" institution existing for the specifically religious needs of men. . . . The Church is thus the restoration by God and the acceptance by man of the original and eternal destiny of creation itself. . . . As institution the Church is in this world the sacrament of the Body of Christ, of the Kingdom of God and the world to come.[15]

Miraculously, sacramentally, mysteriously, invitingly, the horizontal *chronos* can hold the emission of the vertical *kairos* because the swaddled God seems to be kenotically fond of small spaces—like a womb, or a manger, or Hades. The liturgical cult holds him who holds the hourglass in which the liturgical cult takes place. And the world was changed when it received this mystery beating as its heart. It was not changed because one more religious institution had been added, or one more philosophy espoused, or one more moral stoicism suggested; it changed because the original and eternal destiny of creation itself has been restored.

This accounts for a puzzling paradox in the language of the New Testament. The world is good, we have said, and yet worldliness is a sin. How can this be? If the world is good, how can sin enter the picture at all? Can we have too much of goodness? The key must lie in the fact that the root metaphor for sin is "to miss the mark." The *use to which we put* the world may miss the mark, and then the world becomes worldly, just as the body becomes flesh if we put it to the wrong use. We must affirm the good of nature and at the same time reject the natural as our ultimate end. The world becomes worldly when it becomes our end, and not means; the world becomes worldly when it is not a sacramental sign of heaven; the world becomes worldly when it is not put on a liturgical trajectory. Restoration of that liturgical trajectory is an eschatological accomplishment of the Dove, and with his ears we hear the liturgical whoosh. It is witnessed to by monks who have left the world, but not only by them. Everyone will leave the world (either voluntarily, at baptism and monastic vows, or involuntarily, at death) and the only ques-

15. Alexander Schmemann, "Theology and Eucharist," in *Liturgy and Tradition*, 77.

tion will be the state of our souls as we release our grip upon the world. Liturgy teaches us how to die; more than that, as Bouyer wrote, it gives us the power to die:

> Christ died for us, not in order to dispense us from dying, but rather to make us capable of dying efficaciously. . . . Rightly understood, the imitation of Christ is the very essence of the Christian life. We must have in us the mind that Christ had; we must be crucified and buried and rise with him. This, of course, does not mean that we fallen human beings are to copy clumsily the God-man. The whole matter is a mystery signifying that we are to be grafted upon him so that the same life which was in him and which he has come to give us may develop in us as in him and produce in us the same fruits of sanctity and love that it produced in him.[16]

All Christians sacramentally enact this, whatever their state of life.

There is an eschatological sign of the kingdom of God: it is celibacy. The rite for the consecration of a virgin states that it is creating "a sacred person, a transcendent sign of the Church's love for Christ, and an eschatological image of this heavenly Bride of Christ and of the life to come."[17] In addition to this sign, there is also a sacrament of the eschaton: it is marriage. Israel presented Yahweh's covenantal intimacy in marital terms; Jesus used the nuptial feast repeatedly in his parables; the Book of Revelation yearns for the wedding feast of the Lamb when the bride of Christ will meet her husband; and Paul tells us that even in this *aeon* the great mystery of Christ and his Church is seen in Christian marriage. Therefore, the Catechism keeps virginity and marriage side-by-side. "Both the sacrament of Matrimony and virginity for the Kingdom of God come from the Lord himself. It is he who gives them meaning and grants them the grace which is indispensable for living them out in conformity with his will. Esteem of virginity for the sake of the kingdom and the Christian understanding of marriage are inseparable, and

---

16. Louis Bouyer, *The Meaning of the Monastic Life*, xiv and xv.

17. *Catechism of the Catholic Church*, ¶923, quoting the rite *Consecratio virginum, Praenotanda* 1.

they reinforce each other" (CCC ¶1620). Both are liturgical lives. The negation of images and the affirmation of images are inseparable and reinforce each other. In both cases, love is purified until it is hot enough to burn off whatever inhibits transfiguration.

Eschatology is not a place whither we go; it is something that happens. The Christian liturgy is not an escape into otherworldliness; it is finally doing this world, our mundane world, in a way that is free from vice, selfishness, disordered love, idolatry, corruption, and so forth. The white light of Mount Tabor descends upon the altar every eighth day and is prismated from there into the corners of our existence. Liturgy consists of sitting across from God at a festal banquet table. We do so at the altar of the Mass, but the whole cosmos turns out to be a liturgical banquet table, and even that is barely large enough to bear the weight of every rich gift that God is offering, and every responsive sacrifice that we want to return. Olivier Clément said that "the Church is the world in its course of transfiguration."[18] And while the process is slow, sometimes invisible, and certainly demanding, Christian hope knows that it is under way. Yet it must be supported by supernatural aid. Hope is a theological virtue, and Jean Daniélou believes it is the most difficult among the three:

> In spite of the promises of Christ, how many Christians there are who haven't the slightest certainty that they will one day enter into possession of the beatific vision and the overflowing joy of God! How many Christians there are who live without the conviction that they are moving toward this joy! And these people thus show little disposition to generosity because lacking certainty about what is to come, one would rather, as they say, get the most out of this life.[19]

We must enter into conspiracy with the Dove—*con+spire*, breathing together.

---

18. Olivier Clément, *The Roots of Christian Mysticism* (New York: New City Press, 1996), 95.

19. Jean Daniélou, *Prayer: Mission of the Church* (Grand Rapids: Eerdmans Publishing, Company, 1996), 7.

In his little classic, *Portal of the Mystery of Hope,* Charles Péguy imagines faith, hope and love as three sisters:

Faith and love are older;
hope is the youngest and smallest of the three.

The little hope moves forward in between her two older sisters
and one
scarcely notices her.
On the path to salvation, on the earthly path, on the rocky path
of salvation, on the interminable road, on the road in between
her two older sisters, the little hope
Pushes on. . . .
And no one pays attention, the Christian people don't pay
attention,
except to the two older sisters.

[But] It's she, the little one, who carries them all.
Because Faith sees only what is.
But she, she sees what will be.
Charity loves only what is.
But she, she loves what will be.[20]

Hope (which is the embodiment of eschatology) can see what will be, and so empowers both faith and charity. To know the certainty of resurrection, the heart must open to God with a dilation caused by liturgical asceticism across the years of our life. When we celebrate the Paschal accomplishment of our exorcistic reclamation from death to life, from darkness to light, from Satan to God, then our lives become sacrificial. What that means will be discussed in a later chapter, but for now follow the Catechism in using Augustine's definition. "Sacrifice is 'every action done so as to cling to God in communion of holiness, and thus achieve blessedness.'"[21]

Every action. The river of life that John sees flowing from the throne of God and of the Lamb in Revelation 22 does not only satu-

20. Charles Péguy, *The Portal of the Mystery of Hope* (Grand Rapids: Eerdmans Publishing Company, 1996), 9–10.
21. CCC ¶2099, quoting Augustine, *The City of God,* 10.6.

rate our sacramental liturgy, it unstoppably seeps into our personal liturgy to moisten our dry bones for resurrection. When the flood-waters reach their term, then, Augustine says,

> This wholly redeemed city, the assembly and society of the saints, is offered to God as a universal sacrifice by the high priest who in the form of a slave went so far as to offer himself for us in his Passion, to make us the Body of so great a head. . . . Such is the sacrifice of Christians: "we who are many are one Body in Christ." The Church continues to reproduce this sacrifice in the sacrament of the altar so well-known to believers wherein it is evident to them that in what she offers she herself is offered.[22]

He here describes a world on its way to the heavenly Jerusalem, as pictured by the Book of Revelation, which has no temple in the *polis* because the whole *polis* is the temple.

Plato said beauty is the splendor of truth, coming from *splendere*, "to shine." When truth shines, there is beauty. That is why liturgy is beautiful: the Dove tells the world the eschatological truth about itself, i.e., how it should be done, and for what reason it exists, and what is a perfect human being. When that happens, then sacred truth makes the profane beautiful, and the domestic Church glistens splendidly, marriages become sacraments, the cosmos sparkles with sacramental potential, matter elevates to sacrificial orientation, time receives purpose from serving spiritual ends, the poor become an altar of almsgiving (as St. John Chrysostom called them), man and woman are anointed priest and crowned royalty. All names will be restored to their rightful owner at the eschaton, but the liturgy already trains our ear to eavesdrop on this liturgical eschatological *polis*.

---

22. Augustine, *The City of God*, 10.6.

3

The Wing of the Dove

WE KNOW THAT our Christian life should be marked by the liturgy
we celebrate, but how would we account for this, if asked? It would
not be enough to use only natural categories. Anthropological theo-
ries of ritual behavior, sociological models of community influence,
or historical accounts of social development cannot be omitted, but
they are not sufficient to explain the significance of the Church's
liturgical rites. Every society forms the identity of its membership
by means of ritual behavior, but liturgy involves something more,
and if I were to search for a word that could name what that is, the
only appropriate word would be "mystery." When the Christian life
is marked in the liturgy, it is not merely being marked by social
behavior, group dynamic, ritual impact, etc., it is being marked by
an act of God, which is how I propose to understand the term mystery. Mystery is where God acts. That is why the Greek tradition
calls sacraments mysteries, and why a merely horizontal interpretation of liturgy falls short. In the words of Colman O'Neill, "The
Church's visible act of sacramental worship is taken over by Christ
and given value of sanctification quite beyond what it possesses as
an act of Church worship."[1] Christ takes the Church's visible act of
sacramental liturgy into his own hands and gives it an importance
quite beyond what it would possess in our hands alone. In this liturgy the mystery is inscribed upon us, we are raised to heaven on
the wing of the Dove, and we would like to ask about its cost and its
effect.

---

1. Colman O'Neill, O.P., *Meeting Christ in the Sacraments* (New York: Society of
St. Paul/Alba House, 1991), 119.

Lumen Gentium says the Church can be compared "by no weak analogy . . . to the mystery of the incarnate Word" (¶8). In the person of Christ were united divine and human natures in the mystery of the Word made flesh; in the Church, the body of Christ, divine and human actions are united in the mystery of the liturgy. The Holy Spirit puts the Church's prayer into mysterious union with the dialogue between the Son and the Father, and the liturgy is celebrated in mysterious union with Christ's original and ongoing work. The natural worship of the first Adam has value as an exercise of the virtue of religion, but participating in the liturgy of the second Adam has far greater value, because it is participation in the perichoresis of the Trinity. We perform the ritual, but Christ noses his way into it, like a camel into a tent, and mystery arrives. Ritual and rubric only arrange the straw in the manger for the mystery's arrival. What is this mystery, and with what does it mark us? What pattern does it recapitulate in us?

Perhaps going upstream to the origin of liturgy in us would be a helpful way to begin, I mean going to the headwaters of our liturgical life, which is baptism. Our liturgical life originates in the sacraments of Christian initiation, so perhaps there we might catch a glimpse of the liturgical mystery that has been inscribed on us. Over the course of that process of initiation two inscriptions are made. The first inscribes the catechumen's name in the book of the Church at the rite of enrollment, by the bishop's hand; the second is at the other end when the bishop's hand inscribes Christ's mark upon the neophyte's forehead. The rites of initiation unfold between these two, between the time the seeker is enrolled among the catechumens who are calling out for salvation to the Divine One who has been calling to them, and the time the neophyte is enrolled into an order of priestly people who are given power by the Holy Spirit to thereafter concelebrate with Christ his liturgy to the Father. Baptism enrolls us into the liturgical circulation of the Trinity. The mark, the *eikon* imprinted with a chrism oil saturated by the sweet perfume of Christ, was called a *sphragis* by the Greek mystagogues, and a *character* in Latin, from the Greek word *kharax*, which meant a sharp stick that leaves behind an imprint called a *kharakter*. An artist will use a sharp stick in the technique of etching in order to scratch off a waxy covering where he wants a line to appear. Then the plate is washed in acid, which bites into the plate's surface to leave a permanent mark. After the waxy buildup of sin and idolatry has been scratched off during the catechumenate, Christ's mystery can now be marked, etched, engraved, and stamped upon the Christian. The baptismal font is an acid bath! Here is how Louis Bouyer describes what happens to the catechumen when he or she is led to the cosmic waters to be recapitulated (outfitted with a new head):

> The catechumen goes into the water; he plunges into it and disappears completely. When he emerges once more he will no longer be the same man. The dusty image of Adam which he carried before has now been blotted out. He is dead with Christ to the life of man which was spoiled by the devil. Now, washed from his sins, he is a new person in the new Adam. The priestly hand marks his head with holy Chrism, that is the newly-baptized is engraved with the *eikon*, the image of Christ Who is the *eikon* of the Heavenly Father. . . . It is no longer he—his old self—who lives in him; it is Christ who lives in him, the Man of the last times, the Man come down from heaven, the Son of God. And now, through Baptism in water and of the Spirit, the new Christian has been conformed to the Mystery: the divine pattern revealed in Christ has been imprinted in him. [2]

Every succeeding liturgical celebration builds up the likeness of that initial imprint: the liturgy of the hours, the liturgical year, the sacraments, and the Divine Liturgy of the Mass all add layer upon layer to the refreshed *imago Dei*.

Before an iconographer begins painting he inscribes an outline of the figure to the prepared gesso on the board with a pointed tool. Then egg-tempera paint can be applied, adding lighter layers upon darker. This iconographic method was frequently compared to the activity of the Holy Spirit. We know that whatever ascetical work we do to progress toward holiness is only a matter of cooperating with the true iconographer. The saint is written by God's own hand—

2. Louis Bouyer, *Liturgical Piety* (Notre Dame: University of Notre Dame Press, 1955), 167.

auto-graphed by God. The Holy Spirit can accomplish this because although the three persons are distinct in view of their relations, they are one nature or substance (*Catechism of the Catholic Church*, ¶255). Therefore, Cyril of Alexandria patiently explains that the Holy Spirit does not draw upon us a divine beauty that is alien to the one that he himself is, "but rather, being God in proceeding from God, he himself marks the hearts of those who receive him as a seal upon wax. In this way, by the communication of his own life and resemblance, he restores nature according to the beauty of the divine model, and returns to man his resemblance with God."[3] The mystery of Christ's life and death must be repeated in every person who wants to be raised on the wing of the Dove to enter the heavenly sanctuary with Christ. The Holy Spirit is everywhere witnessing to Christ the Word, and it is the mark of the crucified one that the Spirit places on our foreheads like a seal upon wax.

This spiritual iconography was a favorite image of the Fathers of the Church, and following are four examples. First, Methodius says that although we could recognize the king from a sketch, the icon will look more like the king when colors have been added, and this is what Christ came to make possible when he "assumed our human form, a form marred by the scars of many sins, so that we would be enabled to receive his divine form.... He who was God chose to appear in our human flesh so that we could behold, as we do in a painting, a divine model of life, and thus we were made able to imitate the one who painted this picture."[4] Second, Gregory of Nyssa says that our Maker wants "the portrait to resemble His own beauty, by the addition of virtues, as if it were with colors."[5] Third, this is also Ephrem the Syrian's point when he marvels that God "could have forced us to please Him, without any trouble to Himself," but instead he chose to toil by every means "so that we might act pleas-

3. Cyril of Alexandria, *Thesaurus de sancta et consubstantiali Trinitate*, 34 (PG 75, 609). This translation from Josemaría Escrivá, *Christ Is Passing By* (New Rochelle, New York: Scepter Press, 1990), 184.

4. Methodius, Discourse 1, chapter 4, this translation from Christoph Schönborn, *God's Human Face* (San Francisco: Ignatius Press, 1995), 56.

5. Gregory of Nyssa, *On the Making of Man*, ch. 5, section 1, *Nicene and Post-Nicene Fathers*, Vol. 5 (Peabody, MA: Hendrickson Publishers, Inc., 2004), 391.

ingly to Him of our free will, that we might depict our beauty with the colors that our own free will had gathered."[6] Finally, Diadochus of Photiki explains how this is done:

> Painters begin by sketching the outline of a portrait in a single color, then they gradually add the luster of one color to the other until they copy their model, right down to the very hairs of its head. In just such a way, the grace of God in baptism begins by making the image once again what it was when man first came into existence. Then when grace sees us aspiring with our whole will to the beauty of the likeness . . . he adds the luster of one virtue after another, and, by raising the soul's beauty from splendor to splendor, makes it an unmistakable likeness.[7]

God's legislative finger wrote the Ten Commandments into stone tablets given to Moses, and on them, we are told, were all the words God had spoken to Israel from the midst of the fire on that day of assembly (Deuteronomy 9:10). Now God's iconographic finger inscribes the mystery of Christ onto the stoniest of hearts, and thereupon we can find all the words of the apostolic faith spoken to the apostles from the midst of Pentecostal fire. We cannot predict what other ways God will touch human hearts, for the wind blows wherever it pleases (John 3:8), but we can depend upon that strong driving wind coming from the sky to fill the entire house (Acts 2:2) where we assemble for liturgy, because, *Sacrosanctum Concilium* says, the liturgy "is the outstanding means whereby the faithful may express in their lives, and manifest to others, the mystery of Christ and the real nature of the true Church" (SC ¶2). The heavenly whirlwind is waiting to enter the mundane and consecrate it. Fire, Pentecost, wind, transfiguration, sanctification—all evidence of the Dove seeking us out in order to mark us with Christ and raise us with him to the Father above. When we enter the Church we step out of our ordinary world, not because there is anything wrong with that

---

6. Ephrem the Syrian, *Hymns of Faith* 31:1–7, cited in *The Luminous Eye* by Sebastian Brock (Kalamazoo, MI: Cistercian Publications, 1985), 61.

7. Diadochus, *Gnostic Chapters*, n. 89; this translation from Olivier Clément, *The Roots of Christian Mysticism*, 90–91.

world but in order to be taught to see that world in its proper light. In liturgy we practice prayer, thanksgiving, koinonia, opening our hands to receive sacrament and offer sacrifice, and opening our hearts to divine charity, and then, having done the world rightly for one exultant moment, we return to live our daily life in prayer, thanksgiving, and charitable service toward our neighbor. Liturgy is not a hobby, not an escape, not an alternative to life. Liturgy is a rehearsal on a sacred stage for our performance of the mystery in the profane world. By standing uprightly before God at the altar we discover our upright posture in the world. We step across the threshold of the narthex into a sacred realm, so that when we return across that narthex border we bring light with us into the valley of the shadow of death. The mystery of Christ the Head penetrates his mystical body by the saturation of the Holy Spirit, a penetration begun in the baptismal *sphragis* marked iconically upon us by the Dove and continued throughout our mundane liturgical life.

We are not capable of taking an adequate sounding of this mystery because it stretches from alpha to omega, across the Father's entire plan for creation. We talk about the liturgical ocean as if we could walk through it without more than getting our sandals wet, when, actually, it stretches from creation to eschaton, from this day to the apocalypse. When describing this mystery to the Church at Ephesus, Paul begins by locating it in the mind of the Father. It is God's eternal plan. Paul admits that he is the least of the saints, but the mystery was nevertheless made known to him by revelation (Eph. 9:3), namely that "the Gentiles are coheirs, members of the same body, and copartners in the promise in Christ Jesus through the gospel" (9:6). In Christ Jesus "the plan of the mystery hidden from ages past in God" (9:9) has been accomplished. This had been unknown to previous human generations, and it was startling news to the angels, too, according to John Chrysostom. The angels knew that Israel was God's people, as Deuteronomy 32 says, but they could not have anticipated this extension of the mystery to the Gentiles. "God had said He would save His people Israel," Chrysostom says, "but had said nothing about the nations. The angels knew that the nations were called, but could not imagine that they would be called to the same end and would be seated upon the throne of

God."[8] A mystery hidden within God was finally revealed, namely, that the love exchanged in the perichoresis of the Trinity is extended to all of mankind, Jew and Gentile. Moses knew that it involved the former from the moment he received the law on Mount Sinai; Paul did not know it involved the latter until he met the mystery in person on the road to Damascus. We conduct every liturgy on the road to Damascus ourselves, also waiting to meet Christ in person.

John Chrysostom exclaims: "Strange! What friendship! For He tells us His secrets; the mysteries, says [Paul], of His will.... This He desired, this He travailed for, as one might say, that He might be able to reveal to us the mystery. What mystery? *That He would have man seated up on high.*"[9] The mystery has four unfolding chapters. First, it is the plan hidden in the mind of the Father from ages past, the telos embedded in every atom and every soul. Second, it is the economy of salvation across the history of Israel. Third, this plan was hypostasized (made actual in person) as Jesus of Nazareth, the mystery become flesh. And fourth, it is the Mystical Body of Jesus wherein the Holy Spirit enfolds Christ's disciples into spiritual life. The mystery is (i) the Father's will, (ii) Israel's salvation history, (iii) Christ in the flesh, and (iv) Christ's mystical body, the Church with her sacraments. The Father's will, actualized in Christ, served by the Church, results in mankind's exaltation so that God may be glorified. The liturgy has begun.

The historical events in that third moment, the historical life of Christ, are traditionally numbered as four: the Incarnation, Crucifixion, Resurrection, and Ascension. All of them are essential—the middle two especially, because they are the passage through death to life, and I would not like them to be overlooked. However, I will focus now on the neglected first and last of these events in order to emphasize the teleology of the mystery especially visible in the Incarnation and the Ascension. It is unfortunate that we treat the former as simply a means to bring Christ on stage for the main act;

---

8. John Chrysostom, Homily 7 on Ephesians 3:8–11. This translation from Jean Daniélou, *The Angels and Their Mission* (Manchester, NH: Sophia Institute Press, 2009), 37.

9. John Chrysostom, Homily 1 on Ephesians 1:1–3.

and it is equally unfortunate that we treat the latter as an after-thought, an abrupt closure to a story we would not otherwise know how to end. These two dimensions of the mystery are more integral to our liturgy of life than we think. In the Incarnation and Ascension the Son accomplishes his Father's intention to seat humanity up on high, in Chrysostom's words. What does this mean?

Help with this question may be found in what Emile Mersch calls the soteriological argument, namely, that we can understand the mystery by its effects in us. "So truly do we possess all things in common with Him, that from what we are it is possible to infer what He had to be, just as it is possible to see, from what He is, what we in turn are destined one day to be."[10] The mystery is the Father's will, something that Christ was intent on obeying, the same thing that the Holy Spirit is intent on completing in us. The mystery of our deification is our adoption as children, and our being raised up to sit on high in the circulation of love that comprises God's Trinitarian life. Christ is head of the Church, no doubt; but we learn something about the head by examining the life he imparts to his body. The Savior is known by the work of salvation he accomplishes in us. Thus, the mystery of our deification sheds light upon the Incarnation: the mystery of man-made-God sheds light upon the mystery of God-made-man. This is why Georges Florovsky could say that "the doctrine of the Church itself is but an 'extended Christology,' the doctrine of the 'total Christ,' totus Christus, caput et corpus."[11]

Mersch points out numerous instances of this soteriological argument in action. For example, Irenaeus argues that Christ had to possess a material body, since it was human beings he was saving, and

10. Emile Mersch, *The Whole Christ: The Historical Development of the Doctrine of the Mystical Body in Scripture and Tradition* (Milwaukee: The Bruce Publishing Company, 1938), 241. Here are two other formulations of the argument by Mersch: "That we may conclude from what the faithful are to what the Savior is, salvation must be a matter of mystical solidarity between ourselves and Him; we must be able to say in truth that men are saved only in virtue of their incorporation in the Savior" (317). "Indeed, the Incarnation has made Him so like us that we can judge what He is by simply reflecting upon what we ourselves are" (361).

11. Fr. Georges Florovsky, "The Ever-Virgin Mother," in *The Mother of God, A Symposium*, ed. E.L. Mascall (Westminster: Dacre Press, 1959), 52.

human beings are soul and body. And Gregory Nazianzen argues that Christ assumed a rational mind because what was not assumed would not have been healed, and since we have been healed in body and mind, Christ must have assumed both. And Athanasius bases an argument for Christ's divinity upon the divinization of the Christian by saying that if Christ is not consubstantial with the Father, then we are not deified, for how can he communicate to us something that he does not possess in its fullness? If we have only been enlightened, then this Christ must be a great Teacher; if we have only been instructed, then this Christ must be a great Prophet; if we have only been chastened, then this Christ must be a great Law-Giver; but if we are made adoptive sons, then this Christ must be the only begotten Son. How could he share with us a mystery that he was not? Jesus's Incarnation brought to conclusion the secret plan of God to raise men and women and seat them up on high, and it was accomplished in a most surprising way. Irenaeus thinks that even the angels are amazed by the scheme:

> They are not able to search out the wisdom of God, by means of which His handiwork, confirmed and incorporated with His Son, is brought to perfection; that His offspring, the First-begotten Word, should descend to the creature, that is, to what had been molded, and that it should be contained by Him; and, on the other hand, the creature should contain the Word and ascend to Him, passing beyond the angels, and be made after the image and likeness of God.[12]

God's Only Begotten came down from heaven and by the Holy Spirit was incarnate of the Virgin Mary, and by the Holy Spirit creatures rise on the wing of the Dove to God. The descended God is named Jesus, and the ascending humanity is named the Church, and although it includes members of the invisible Church, no one could have recognized the mystery of the Church until the Incarnation happened and the Church was made sacrament. The Incarnation that accomplishes this is not a proposition for our reason to

---

12. Irenaeus, *Against Heresies*, Book V, Chapter 36.

accept as historical fact or dogmatic proposition, it is a reality for our souls to imbibe in liturgy.

Our deification is twinned to Christ's Incarnation. Mankind enters into the life of God because of his hypostatic union, which is the source of the deifying mysteries (the sacraments) that touch our whole being. They come forth from Christ's humanity to ours, body to body. I had this in mind when I defined liturgy as the Trinity kenotically extending its life to us, with all the graces we need to enter that life. I was trying to describe liturgy as a royal highway between the Trinity and man, an avenue down which the Father extends his love incarnate (through the Holy Spirit), and up which the believer is drawn in hopeful faith (through the Holy Spirit).[13] But I did not understand the full consequence of my own definition because I was thinking of the Incarnation as one act and the Ascension occurring thirty years later. But what if this one avenue has two-way traffic on it? What if the Incarnation is bipartite? What if Incarnation and Ascension are not separated by chronology but united by mystery? I am stirred to this idea by Charles Williams's underscoring the way of affirmation by means of the creed attributed to Athanasius. "The maxim of this way is in the creed of Saint Athanasius: 'not by conversion of the Godhead into flesh, but by taking of the Manhood into God.'"[14]

Humility protests that we are moving in the wrong direction. The Incarnation, we will say, is Christ coming down (*kenosis*), whereas this formulation speaks of man being brought up. But we must not speculate like philosophers upon a hypothetical move by the deity,

---

13. Virgil Michel provides a definition of liturgy that involves the activity of the Trinity, and I have not seen any better. "The liturgy, through Christ, comes from the Father, the eternal source of the divine life in the Trinity. It in turn addresses itself in a special way to the Father, rendering him the homage and the glory of which it is capable through the power of Christ. The flow of divine life between the eternal Father and the Church is achieved and completed through the operation of the Holy Ghost. The liturgy, reaching from God to man, and connecting man to the fullness of the Godhead, is the action of the Trinity in the Church. The Church in her liturgy partakes of the life of the divine society of the three persons in God." *The Liturgy of the Church, according to the Roman Rite* (New York: Macmillan, 1937), 40.

14. Williams, *The Figure of Beatrice*, 9.

we must let the celebrated mystery condition our thinking. We stand as liturgists face to face with the God made flesh. What happens in such an encounter? We are lifted up to God. Augustine feels these effects even when encountering Jesus in the Eucharist:

> When first I knew you, you raised me up so that I could see that there was something to be seen, but also that I was not yet able to see it. I gazed on you with eyes too weak to resist the dazzle of your splendor. Your light shone upon me in its brilliance, and I thrilled with love and dread alike. I realized that I was far away from you. It was as though I were in a land where all is different from your own and I heard your voice calling from on high, saying "I am the food of full-grown men. Grow and you shall feed on me. But you shall not change me into your own substance, as you do with the food of your body. Instead you shall be changed into me."[15]

Augustine has described the position of every one of us, every week, before every altar. And what friendship! we exclaim with Chrysostom again. God would have us seated up on high, where our weak eyes will be filled with his brilliant light, and we will rise on the wing of the Dove to be thrilled with the overwhelming love of God. The end result of his descent is our ascent. Therefore, Chrysostom says in his third homily on Ephesians, "Two things He has done, the greatest things. He has both Himself descended to the lowest depth of humiliation, and has raised up man to the height of exaltation."[16] This is the motion of our entire liturgical life, in sacrament and in each person.

We are familiar enough with the historical fact that the Son of God has descended to us in the Incarnation, but we are less familiar with the sacramental fact that this works our ascent. Jean Daniélou reminds us of this latter consequence of the Incarnation by calling our attention to a particular Greek verb in a passage from St. Hilary. The Church Father writes, "The only Son of God is born a man of the Virgin Mary, to achieve in his own person the elevation

---

15. Augustine, *Confessions*, book 7, ch. 10, translation by R. S. Pine-Coffin (New York: Penguin Books, 1961), 147.

16. Chrysostom, Homily 3 on Ephesians, ch. 1, verses 15–20.

(*prokope*) of man to God in the fullness of time."[17] *Prokope* means elevation, advancement, ascent, or progress and the Incarnation consists of both *kenosis* and *prokope*. Christ's Incarnation elevates, it makes advancement towards God possible, it gives progress to our ascent. The single mystery is bipartite, and if its first motion occurred at Nazareth, the second motion is still occurring in every liturgy and elevates our lives. Daniélou summarizes:

> By [the hypostatic union] the purpose of mankind's existence is completely achieved. In the first place, mankind enters upon the life of God. The grace of the hypostatic union, belonging as of right to the Son in person, is the source of deification for all who belong to him. So, for St. Paul, and for the Fathers of the fourth and fifth centuries who borrowed his language, Christ is the "first-fruits" of sanctified humanity. Gregory of Nyssa, in particular, developed this line of thought, against Apollinaris. "In the last days, the Word of God, uniting himself to the lowliness of our human nature, is made flesh for the love of man, and being made one with mankind has taken the whole of human nature into him-self, so that mankind should be deified in him through this union with the Godhead, the whole mass being sanctified through these firstfruits." This deification of mankind is the destiny for which the race was providentially intended.[18]

Another translation of the phrase upon which Williams focused can go this way: "Not by conversion of the Godhead into flesh; but by *assumption* of the Manhood by God" (*sed assumptione humanitatis in Deum*). The emptying makes the assumption possible. If I may dare say it, Christ assumes human nature in two ways: Christ took it on (*kenosis*) and Christ took it up (*prokope*).

And now Christology meets Mariology. At her Assumption human nature was perfected and achieved its purpose. Alongside the incarnate divine hypostasis, there can be a deified human hypostasis. The reason why the Church has pursued mariological

---

17. Jean Daniélou, *The Lord of History* (New York: Longmans, Green & Co., 1958), 191.
18. Ibid., 192.

doctrines is to understand the fullness of the Incarnation. Vladimir Lossky says that the supreme vocation of created beings is to have by grace what God has by nature, so "if the Mother of God could realize [this], in her human and created person . . . then the destiny of the Church and the world has already been reached, not only in the uncreated person of the Son of God but also in the created person of his Mother."[19] This destiny had already been reached in Jesus, risen and ascended, but the question remained whether it can be shared with other human beings. How deep does the mark of this mystery go? Jesus is unique, but will he remain alone?[20] Olivier Clément suggests the depths are plumbed by our spiritual life of liturgy. "All the mysteries of the Gospel are not only performed in the liturgy but take possession of us in the spiritual life. The Word is continually being born in the stable of our heart. . . . To ensure this birth of Christ in us is the true function of liturgical times and seasons, interpreted inwardly by ascesis, prayer and contemplation."[21] Jesus stands at the head of mankind's *prokope*, leading it further up and further in; and immediately behind him comes Mary; and in her train, gathered in the arms of *Mater Ecclesia*, comes the whole Church. By the power of the Holy Spirit the Son of God was made man; can the power of that same Spirit make us sons of God? Yes. That is why Stratford Caldecott claims that "In the West our theology of the Spirit has tended to take the form of mariology."[22]

While the angels were rolling back the stone from the tomb, Christ was unhinging the gates of Hades, trampling down death by death. The angels rolled back the stone so they could let liturgy out. Man's ascension into Godhood was made possible by Christ's Incarnation into manhood, a result Solovyov calls Godmanhood.[23] This

---

19. Lossky, "Panagia," *The Mother of God*, 34.

20. I am aware of the antinomy: to be unique means to be alone, but Christ apophatically violates the rules of logic. Alongside "sober inebriation," and "bright darkness," we have "unique but not alone."

21. Clément, *The Roots of Christian Mysticism*, 251.

22. Stratford Caldecott, "The Final Mystery," *Logos: A Journal of Catholic Thought and Culture*, 3, no. 3 (2000): 87–108.

23. Vladimir Solovyov, *Lectures on Godmanhood* (Semantron Press, 2007).

is our spiritual life, the wing of the Dove raising us spiritually. Christ drained the swamp of death, and replaced it with a life-giving river (described in the Book of Revelation) that runs all the way from the empty tomb to the "Today" in which we stand. Only the Holy Spirit can operate in these depths; only the Holy Spirit can permeate breath and bone; only the life-giving Spirit animates our liturgical life.

There is two-way traffic in the liturgical mystery. The Son of God came down and something went up; the Son of Man went up and something came down. At his Incarnation, Christ descended and human nature was elevated; at his Ascension, Christ's human nature rose to heaven and down came new life in the Spirit, Pentecost, the Church. These two kisses—heaven bending down to earth and earth straining upward to heaven—compose the liturgical mystery. The Holy Spirit was involved in each of them. At every liturgy there is a meeting of the descent of God and the ascent of man. At every liturgy there is the Son and the Dove. The Incarnation punctured the roof between heaven and earth, the Ascension punctured the ceiling between earth and heaven. Christ as Lord comes down to us in priest, assembly, scripture, and Eucharist, and Christ as brother leads us up in prayer, sacrifice, thanksgiving, praise, and glorification of the Father.

If the result of the Incarnation is Godmanhood, then even though Christ's historical *kenosis* happened only once, so long as Godmanhood is propagated and prolonged we might dare say the Incarnation continues. Mersch does. "The hypostatic union does not affect our Lord alone," he writes, "but it is somehow prolonged in us, the members; we are the prolongation of the Head, and the hypostatic union renders us divine by reason of our continuity with the God-man."[24] And, "this same hypostatic union causes to flow into our human nature the life that it imparts to the humanity of Christ."[25] This is what mediatorship means. Whereas Jesus is our brother, sharing our human nature; and whereas Jesus's divine nature is the Logos, in union with the Father; therefore Jesus causes

24. Emile Mersch, *The Whole Christ* (Milwaukee: Bruce, 1938), 283.
25. Ibid., 356.

to flow into our human nature the life that the Logos imparts to Jesus's own humanity. What occurred in his historical body is experienced by his mystical body, which is why he is source of the liturgy that we celebrate, and all the sacraments flow from his humanity. This is our synergistic participation in the Trinity's perichoresis, which Daniélou calls the mystery of Christianity in its entirety:

> This is the heart and core of the irreducible originality of Christianity, that the Son of God came among us to reveal these two intimately related truths: that there is within God himself a mysterious living love, called the Trinity of Persons; and that in and through the Son we men are called to share this life of love. *The mystery of the Holy Trinity, known to us through the Word made flesh, and the mystery of the deification of man in him—that is the whole of our religion,* summed in one person, the person of Jesus Christ.[26]

Kenosis and *prokope* are mirror-imaged. The Incarnation is reflected in the Ascension and Pentecost.

We may understand Christ's cross and resurrection to be the completion of his Incarnation. And we may understand Pentecost to be a completion of his Ascension. Christ's *kenosis* was not finished at the manger, because he had to take one step further down in order to find man and woman where they are—in Hades. And when his *kenosis* finally breaks the vacuum seal of Hades an epicletic cry escapes from our lips: Come Holy Spirit. An *epiclesis* is human petition and divine concession. It is the divine will conceding to human petition. We can perform our part of the liturgy with confidence because the Spirit helps our weakness and intercedes for us with groanings too deep for words (Romans 8:26). The gift of *epiclesis* is one of Christ's most precious endowments to his Church. Come upon us and bring us back to life; come upon this catechumen, this confirmand, this ordinand and give them the spirit of *diakonia;* come upon our lives and make them pure sacrifice; come upon the face of the earth and renew it; come and give us hearts made of flesh, not stone. We set out bread and wine on the altar, as Gideon put wool fleece on the threshing floor (Judges 6), and ask

---

26. Daniélou, *The Lord of History,* 118. Emphasis added.

God to send down his Spirit on them like the dewfall, making the matter we set out into sacrament. All *epicleses* in the Church's celebrations of the mystery are responses to Christ's *kenosis*. Because he went to the cross, we can beg the Holy Spirit to come upon our memorial of that sacrifice. Because he breathed upon the apostles, we can beg the Holy Spirit to come upon their successors, the bishops. Because he went down into the Jordan, we can beg the fountain of baptism to be graciously unsealed for the Church in that font. The fire of Pentecost happened as a backdraft of Christ's ascension, and in it we welcome the descent of the Church, the sacraments, the priesthood, and everything required for us to live the mystery from now until its fulfillment.

Godmanhood must be recapitulated in each one of us, and for that purpose we have a Divine Pedagogue to teach us. Christ shows us the pattern of emptying and elevating so that these movements may occur in us. Our liturgy is patterned after Christ, except, Nicholas Cabasilas reminds us, we sinners do not observe the same order as our Lord:

> We are joined to Him who for our sake was incarnate and who deified our nature, who died and rose again. *Why then do we not observe the same order as He, but begin where He left off and reach the end where He began?* It is because He descended in order that we might ascend. It is by the same path that it was His task to descend, that it is ours to ascend. As in the case of a ladder, that which was His last step as he descended is for us the first step as we ascend. It could not be otherwise because of the very nature of things.[27]

The pattern of Jesus is repeated in our liturgical life, except it is repeated in reverse order because he is being incarnated and we are being deified. Christ's *kenosis* consisted of putting away glory, and our *kenosis* consists of putting away the old Adam. Christ emptied himself in order to take up humanity, and we lay down sinful humanity in order to take up divine life. Christ veiled the glory that

27. Nicholas Cabasilas, *The Life in Christ* (Crestwood, NY: St. Vladimir's Seminary Press, 1974), 66. Emphasis added.

was rightfully his, and we turn away from self-glorification. The only begotten Son became a slave, and we slaves become adopted sons. We follow him along the same path, but his last step is our first step.

And where is that step, that bottom rung to which he descended and from which we begin our ascent? It is the place where the Incarnation took the Son of Man: Golgotha. By his death, Jesus completed his mission of becoming man; but by our death we begin our ascent on the wing to resurrected life. Athanasius set up the extended syllogism: God had bestowed on Adam his own life, but man turned to things corruptible by counsel of the devil; repentance was not enough because corruption could not be got rid of except through death; being immortal, God could not die, and for this reason he assumed a body capable of death.[28] Jesus's face was set toward Jerusalem from the moment of his birth. It was the final step to be taken, and Christ took it in order to change death. Now death is no longer a step of descent into Hades, it can be the first step of ascent into Heaven. As Louis Bouyer says, "Christ died for us, not in order to dispense us from dying, but rather to make us capable of dying efficaciously."[29] What a witness Christians would be to the world if each one of us died with power. Every liturgy must be stretched taut upon the cross in order to be valid. The life that arises out of our daily death ought to be attractive to everyone who sees it, and if it is not, then we are not doing our death properly. It has not reached perfection. That is what liturgical asceticism in our daily life is for. That is why we have been inscribed with the cross and capacitated to mimic the Son when he loved the Father before all things. The Son loved the Father's glory more than his own happiness, more than his own life; the Son loved all things for the sake of the Father; and if we were to do Christian liturgy in the Spirit of Christ, then the Holy Spirit would have to carve this selflessness into our hearts until we desire only one thing. Augustine said purity of heart is to will one thing. And purity of heart is how John Cassian

---

28. Athanasius, *On the Incarnation of the Word*, ch. 15.

29. Louis Bouyer, *The Paschal Mystery: Meditations on the Last Three Days of Holy Week* (Chicago: Henry Regnery Co., 1950), xiv.

translated Evagrius's term *apatheia* (dispassion). Blessed are the pure in heart, for they shall see God (Matthew 5:8).

The final purpose of liturgy is to glorify God, and the prototype of such a life of liturgy is Christ himself. He is the primordial liturgist, and we are his apprentices. Therefore, what is required on our part is more than philosophical assent or moral mimicry. We are not following Socrates or Marcus Aurelius: we are following the Son of God. This discipleship is *Sequela Christi*, and Ratzinger explains the difference:

> Sequela Christi does not mean: imitating the man Jesus. This type of attempt would necessarily fail—it would be an anachronism. The Sequela of Christ has a much higher goal: to be assimilated into Christ, that is to attain union with God.... Man is not satisfied with solutions beneath the level of divinization.... The Sequela of Christ is not a question of morality, but a "mysteric" theme—an ensemble of divine action and our response.[30]

Liturgy is an ensemble of divine action and our response. If that ensemble disintegrates, then liturgy becomes ritual, asceticism becomes morality, Christianity becomes just another religion, mysticism becomes spiritual enthusiasm, theology becomes philosophy of religion, eschatology becomes a species of human hope, providence becomes luck, and the temple becomes a meeting hall for the Jesus Club.

Humanity is not satisfied with solutions beneath the level of divinization, said Ratzinger. Neither is humankind satisfied with rituals beneath the level of divinization, I conclude, nor with evangelization strategies that stop short of divinization, nor with catechetics that point to anything other than divinization, nor with any activity of the Church drained of this mystery. All people thirst for the infinite, which is why any end offered to man or woman will fail them if it does not lead to the finale of liturgical life. Liturgy is in-Godding.

---

30. Joseph Cardinal Ratzinger, "The New Evangelization," II.3. Jubilee for Catechists, December 10, 2000. http://www.ewtn.com/new_evangelization/Ratzinger.htm.

We already live in the last times; this is our ecclesial identity. The mystery entered history and has performed like a current in the river, directing mankind to the mystery made flesh. Jean Corbon picks up the imagery of the Book of Revelation to describe liturgy as a river of life that flows from the throne of God. We would not have known anything about this river if the Son himself had not revealed it to us (John 1:18). It is pictured by the "seer of Patmos" when he

> glimpses the indescribable energy of the Blessed Trinity at the heart of the messianic Jerusalem, that is, this Church of the last times, in which we are now living. If we let the river of life permeate us, we become trees of life, for the mystery that the river symbolizes takes hold of us. This is the mystery above all others, the one in which Saint Paul sees and contemplates the entire saving plan, which the living God is carrying out in history. We too, who stand at the threshold of its complete fulfillment, are allowed to apprehend by faith its beginning and unfolding.[31]

If we let the river of life permeate us, we stand like sentries along its passage through the mundane. As Christ proved to Thomas, the spear's penetration still slits his side, and from it the mysteries (sacraments) flood the world when his resurrected humanity celebrates the heavenly liturgy as eternal priest. The sacraments do not stand between us and Jesus like a wall; they extend from Jesus to us like a bridge. They cross the centuries and lift us out of historical, worldly time to set us into eternal, resurrected encounter. His life is overlaid on ours, his habits become ours, his responses to his Father become our second nature, and his incarnating descent makes possible our deifying ascent. He gives us his Spirit toward this end, and we bear the Dove's mark. The liturgy sacramentally presents Christ so that his mystery can be recapitulated in each individual Christian, who becomes by grace what Christ is by nature. Liturgy is the life of the Trinity extended to us (*kenosis*) for the purpose of bringing about our elevation (*prokope*).

This ascent on the wing of the Dove, this *prokope* will require a cooperative response on our part, one which I consider to be asceti-

---

31. Corbon, *Wellspring of Worship*, 29.

cism in its fullest meaning. This is not the asceticism of personal improvement; this is not moral asceticism; this is not even religious asceticism. It is liturgical asceticism: an asceticism birthed from, formed by, and at the service of the liturgical mysteries. John Behr describes asceticism's hammer-blows as a kind of sculpting. "We are a work in progress; our blueprint, the statue lying in the block of marble waiting to be sculpted, is already in the image of Christ, though for now hidden with him. We are being worked on, so that when he appears, we will appear with him."[32] The first nature, which we must kill, has to be split open so that the seed of new life can be planted and find its way to the surface.

On the one hand, in his mercy God does not require that our asceticism be finished before he will grant us entry into his temple; on the other hand, in his justice God does not leave the unclean lips of a sinful man untouched by his holy fire. Because our God is a God of both mercy and justice, we live a rhythm of liturgy and asceticism. His mercy permits us to celebrate the Eucharist while we are still incomplete, and his justice will not leave us alone until we are co-sons with his Son. By the power of the Holy Spirit he became man; by the power of that same spirit we become divine. In the liturgical mysteries we receive training for our ascent to God the Father, alongside our brother Christ, whose icon the Dove has autographed on our brow. Then our daily life is marked with an incredible freedom made possible by our adoption and deification. Matthias Scheeben says that natural man does not have the obligation or right to know anything more than his duty to honor God and subject himself to God, and for this it is sufficient to know that God exists, is infinite, is all-powerful, etc.—things that philosophy of religion knows about God by natural reason. But God has higher beings in view, and "If [man] is admitted to these mysteries, he thereby enters into a certain friendship with God; for only to friends does anyone reveal his most intimate secrets. He ascends far beyond his native lowliness and, initiated into the secrets of his

---

32. John Behr, "The Eschatological Dimensions of Liturgy," *Assembly: a Journal of Liturgical Theology* 36, no. 1 (January 2010): 2–9, at 3.

Lord, feels himself summoned to all the other privileges as well as to the duties of a true friend."[33]

To repeat Chrysostom one final time: what friendship! God desires man seated up on high, and invites his friends into the perichoresis of Trinitarian life. Jesus reveals this mystery by accomplishing it; that is the only way it could be revealed. The mystery is not a piece of information to be considered like a fact, it is an offer of life to be ingested like a supernatural food. Jesus communicates the revelation by taking us into the revelation. That is why it cannot be known in the abstract, by academic theology: it must be known by experience, by liturgical theology (*theologia prima*). Jesus no longer calls us servants, because a servant does not know the master's business; he calls us friends, for everything he learned from his Father he has made known to us (John 15:15); and he wants to make men and women sons like himself. Liturgy is the extension of the Trinity's perichoresis, the accomplishment of our deification, an opportunity for self-emptying that will glorify God the way Christ's own *kenosis* glorified his Father in Heaven.

It feels impossible. We feel ourselves to be too heavy, too stubborn for this subtle, agile ascent. Our feet do not seem trained for heaven, our eyes remain downcast, our hands are idle, and our mind is distracted by the world (a state called "worldliness"). Paul Claudel says, "I feel that I have undertaken something beyond my strength. These wings of wood, how can I adjust them to sit on my shoulders?"[34] He speaks truly. It is beyond our strength. The strength must be given to us mysteriously: I mean, given to us by means of the mysteries. That liturgy is mysterious does not mean it is "cryptic" or "enigmatic," it means that liturgy is founded upon grace. It brings us a life lived from the power of Christ, not lived from our own power. The mark of the mystery upon us is a cross. It is fitted on us as wings by which we may join the Dove in full flight. And when the cross is properly adjusted upon our shoulders, then

33. Matthias Scheeben, *The Mysteries of Christianity* (St. Louis: B. Herder Book Co., 1946), 126–28.

34. Paul Claudel, *I Believe in God: a Meditation on the Apostles' Creed* (New York: Holt, Rinehart and Winston, Inc., 1963), 52.

suddenly, surprisingly, *kenosis* becomes *prokope*, self-emptying is the way to our deepest fulfillment, death becomes life, Incarnation is Ascension, Ascension is Pentecost, and human beings fall upward under the force of the Holy Spirit's rising wing. Then death will work the way it should have worked for Adam, did work for Christ, and could work for a saint: it becomes a path to life. Liturgical asceticism is only the compression of the spring and its release is our elevation. Having exhaled over the waters of creation (both in Genesis and at the baptismal font), the Father will inhale again, drawing all things back to himself. The Spirit is fire, which came down upon the Church at Pentecost, but fire's appetite is to ascend and when it does, we can join Elijah on his fiery shuttle. If the prototype for our life of liturgy is Christ himself, then in the celebration of the liturgy the Dove will mark us with the mystery of Christ's own *kenosis*, to invite our synergistic flight into deification.

4

The Eye of the Dove

THE WAY WE THINK about things is determined by the metaphors we use, metaphors embedded in us so deeply that we often don't notice them. Our modern metaphor for sight is the camera. It is literal *photo-graphe*, "writing with light," because light is bouncing off every object in the room and ricocheting into a lens opened for only a fraction of a second in order to scratch the film. Light comes through the camera lens from the outside, and when we borrow that metaphor to explain sight, we think of light coming from the outside through the lens of our eye, opened for a faction of a second, in order to scratch our retina. In the philosophy of optics this is called the *intromission theory*. Light bounces off the book cover to passively implant an image in our eye that will then be transferred to our mind. As the famous saying goes, there is nothing in the mind that was not first in the senses, and epistemology has used the sense of sight more than any of the other four senses when reflecting upon (apologies for the pun) how objects, and then concepts, "get into the mind." Light plays a role in mediating noumena to us as visual phenomena. Some ancient Greek philosophers had already maintained a version of this intromission theory, and suggested that objects cast copies of themselves upon the eye.

However, there was another theory alongside this understanding, called the *emission theory*. This theory proposed that light did not travel from the outside in, but from the inside out. The eye was the source of the light by which the eye itself saw. In the 5th century BC the Greek philosopher Empedocles said the eyes were like a lantern, blazing with a special kind of fire, casting forth an inner light that emanated outwards, and whatever the light hit was instantly seen. The combined influence of Plato, Ptolemy, and Galen kept this idea in play for thousands of years. Granted, this emission theory finally lost out as the science of optics continued to develop, from Bacon to Newton to the understanding of photons in modern physics, but it is interesting to notice how this now out-of-date metaphor can still ably express certain experiences. The ancient physicians spoke of "an active eye" and, indeed, sight is the most aggressive of the senses: it does not have to wait for objects to come within contact or closer range, as does the ear, nose, tongue, and fingertip. Instead, sight leaps out across distances, seizes its object, and pulls a mental copy into the mind. This gives looking a violent character if it is done without permission, and is what makes voyeurism creepy. Certain English phrases have continued to reflect this emission theory: "a fire in his eye," "bright eyes," "his eyes grew dim," or "the twinkling of an eye." We have an "outlook." What Aristotle meant by an "eyebeam" can be easily understood by us when we hear Charles Dickens say "With affection beaming in one eye."

I am not interested in restoring the emission theory as a science of *natural* optics. I'm more interested in its usefulness in helping us to imagine a *supernatural* optics. When we think about the liturgy of the world, might the metaphor of a lighthouse have an advantage over the metaphor of a camera? What if liturgical sight were a matter of light pouring forth from the eye and illuminating our world? What if liturgical sight were a matter of seeing by the light of the Holy Spirit, who indwells the liturgist since baptism, so that we, ourselves, see with the eye of the Dove? "Behold, you are fair, My love! behold, you are fair! You have dove's eyes" (Song of Solomon 1:15). Here is Gregory Palamas's description, himself no stranger to controversies concerning divine light and the energies of God:

> Man's sight, when it is in action, itself *becomes light, communes with the light and sees with it,* and the first thing it beholds is this light poured out on everything visible. In exactly the same way, anyone fortunate enough to attain to the divine energy, and to undergo divine transformation, himself becomes completely like the light. He is with the light, and by means of it sees clearly things

which, were it not for this great and inexpressible grace, would be invisible to all.[1]

The liturgical sight of those fortunate enough to come in contact with the divine energy is transformed, and the person himself becomes like the light, by means of which he can see the world. I am calling this "mundane liturgical theology" because it is a theology that makes the Christian see the mundane world liturgically. We might even say that it gives the Christian a different world to see. Wittgenstein remarked in passing that "the world of the happy man is a different one from that of the unhappy man."[2] Of course, there is a state of affairs outside of us that we are given, but he is here thinking of the world we create by a good or bad exercise of the will. In that manner, I am saying that the world of the liturgical person is completely different from the world of the idolater. If, on the one hand, holiness and love emanate from our eye to seize everything for the kingdom of God, then the liturgical person sees a dawn instead of a twilight, a pathway to life instead of a dead end, his neighbor as Christ knocking, and his daily life filled with moments of providence to be obeyed instead of strikes of fate to be endured. If, on the other hand, the light of liturgy is not in us as an eyebeam, then matter loses sacramentality, history is emptied of providence, the stars move further away, my neighbor is a grievance, the spiritual is a nuisance, and my sickness is unto death.

The liturgical rites detonate an explosion, but the radiation from these sacramental outbursts is not intended to be contained by the blast walls of the sanctuary. Paul Evdokimov speaks of sacraments as an action of "punching holes" in a world we have closed off to God (the original sin). They "devulgarize" the world we have constructed in our own image, and teach us

> that everything is destined for a liturgical fulfillment. . . . The final destiny of water is to participate in the mystery of the Epiphany; of wood, to become a cross; of the earth, to receive the body of the

---

1. Gregory Palamas, *Mary the Mother of God: Sermons by St. Gregory Palamas* (South Canaan, PA: Mount Thabor Publishing, 2005), 48. Emphasis added.
2. Ludwig Wittgenstein, *Tractatus* 6.43 (London: Rutledge & Kegan Paul, 1961), 72.

Lord during his rest on the Sabbath. . . . Olive oil and water attain their fullness as conductor elements for grace on regenerated man. Wheat and wine achieve their ultimate *raison d'etre* in the eucharistic chalice. . . . A piece of being becomes a hierophany, an epiphany of the sacred. . . .

Nothing in the world remains foreign to [Christ's] humanity, everything has received the seal of the Holy Spirit. This is why the Church in turn blesses and sanctifies all of creation. . . . Cosmic matter thus becomes a conductor of grace, a vehicle of the divine energies.[3]

The structure of the Church is designed to run in a straight line from the sanctuary, through the nave, and out the narthex: a linear structure that directs the force of the liturgical explosion onto the street. Alexander Schmemann calls this the true subject matter of liturgical theology. The true subject matter of liturgical theology is not simply what happens in the sanctuary but its encounter with the mundane street. He reminisces in a journal entry about the days of his youth in Paris when he would pass by the Church of St. Charles of Monceau within which a silent Mass was being said. And what was the effect on him?

The street, as it was, acquired a new charm that was understandable and obvious only to me, who knew at that moment the Presence, the feast revealed in the Mass nearby. This experience remains with me forever: a very strong sense of "life" in its physical, bodily reality, in the uniqueness of every minute and of its correlations with life's reality. At the same time, this interest has always been rooted solely in the correlation of all of this with what the silent Mass was a witness to, and reminder of, the presence and the joy. What is that correlation? It seems to me that I am quite unable to explain and determine it, although *it is actually the only thing that I talk and write about ("liturgical theology")*. It is not an "idea": I feel repulsed by "ideas"; I have an ever-growing conviction that Christianity cannot be expressed by "ideas". . . . This correlation is a tie, not an idea; an experience. It is the experience of the world and life literally in the light of the Kingdom of God,

3. Paul Evdokimov, *Art of the Icon: A Theology of Beauty* (Redondo Beach, CA: Oakwood, 1990), 117.

revealed through everything that makes up the world: colors, sounds, movements, time, space—concrete, not abstract. When this light, which is only in the heart, only inside us, falls on the world and on life, then all is illumined, and the world becomes a joyful sign, symbol, expectancy.[4]

Mundane liturgical theology is that tie between Church and world. According to Schmemann, theology is more a vision than a cogitation: it is the discovery that life in the world should be lived in the light of the Kingdom of God. This Kingdom resides at the deepest foundation of our hearts, but requires of us an ascetical discipline to uncover. Isaac of Syria said, "The ladder of the Kingdom is within you, hidden in your soul. Plunge deeply within yourself, away from sin, and there you will find steps by which you will be able to ascend."[5] This depth plunge is a matter of liturgical asceticism, required before we can arrive at an affirmation of images in the world.

The history of the world's salvation occurs over three acts: namely, creation, fall, and deification. We might name these acts *mnesis*, amnesia, and *anamnesis*, because we were created to be mindful of God, sin is amnesia, and redemption is man's memory restored. In the first act, man and woman are created to exercise a capacity for spiritual sight in a physical world, which Symeon the New Theologian described as seeing with two eyes and two lights:

> Know then that you are double
> and that you possess two eyes,
> the sensible and the spiritual.
> Since there are also two suns
> there is also a double light,
> sensible and spiritual,
> and if you see them, you will be the man
> as you were created in the beginning to be.[6]

---

4. Alexander Schmemann, *The Journals of Father Alexander Schmemann* 1973–1983 (Crestwood: St. Vladimir's Seminary Press, 2002), 13. Emphasis added.

5. Isaac the Syrian, *The Ascetical Homilies of Saint Isaac the Syrian* (Boston: Holy Transfiguration Monastery, 1984), 11.

6. Symeon the New Theologian, *Hymns of Divine Love,* trans. George A. Maloney (Denville, NJ: Dimension Books, 1976), 123.

Man is a hybrid with binocular vision. He has a spiritual eye, by which he can see things the animals can't; and he has a sensible eye, by which he can see things the angels can't; and when human beings work their two eyes together they have a depth perception that other creatures don't possess. This unique position permits man and woman to be cosmic priests of the visible world (a position neither the angel nor the animal can occupy) because man and woman add the splendor of created matter to the celestial praise of God. They are the tongue that gives voice to ontological *logike*. These cosmic priests are made from the clay of the earth yet possess a heavenly light in their eye in order to conduct worship in both spheres. If, in the process of redemption, they are restored and recapitulated as the persons they were created in the beginning to be, this will not mean arriving at the incorporeality of an angel. Christian perfection is not marked by the steady loss of our bodily self. Asceticism is never at the expense of aesthetics.

The second act in the cosmic drama is our fall, our amnesia, our going blind in one eye. Symeon says,

> If you see the sensible sun
> and not the spiritual sun,
> you are really half dead.
> He who is half dead is also a corpse,
> for he is without activity in all domains.[7]

We did not completely lose our spiritual eye in original sin; that is impossible. The *imago Dei* cannot be destroyed because no one can countermand the Creator's ontological act. Since Satan is not an anti-God equipped with a power equal and opposite to the true God, therefore he cannot destroy what God has created, and therefore our image of God can never be lost. But we must realistically admit that the light of our spiritual eye has been dimmed, it is now out of focus, it is distracted to inferior objects. Recall the experience of looking through a window as night falls. We can look through a window to the backyard when there is more light outside than inside, but when the sunlight fades, and there is more light inside

7. Ibid.

than outside, then we see our own reflection in the window. *Incurvatus in se* happened when the lighting in Eden went funny. Creation was no longer a window of theophany when we no longer looked through it but rather looked upon it in the light of self-idolatry. The whole narrative of the fall expresses the experiential evidence we feel daily that we aren't quite the person we were created in the beginning to be. A creature with free will, subject to the seduction of Satan, can all too easily find his eyes clouded with sin's opacity. The passions of vainglory, envy, and anger dull the lights of humility, charity, and meekness. He who is half dead, says Symeon, is already a corpse: there are some virtuous domains in which he is without activity.

Like Samson, we have been blinded in Philistia. Coventry Patmore told us at the end of chapter 1 that Philistia should be glad of God, and it is the mystery of iniquity that there is no longer rejoicing in Philistia. How can the world, which is good, make us worldly? How can a gift of God be a cause of sin? Gnosticism took the easy way out and pitted the corporeal against the incorporeal, but Christianity refuses to follow this cheap lead because it knows the problem to be spiritual, not material. It is a problem in our hearts, not in the cosmos. Creation has not fallen, and creation is not the cause of our fall. Still, creation has suffered the effects of our fall. There is nothing wrong with the world at which we look, but there is something wrong with how we look at that world. We have inherited amblyopia from Adam and Eve, and the eye that has become lazy is our spiritual one. We let our wandering eye rest not on creation's true teleology, but only upon its usefulness to our own self-satisfaction. The world becomes worldly when we do not use our spiritual and sensible eyes together. That accounts for why Christian doctrine must walk the paradox of simultaneously affirming the good of nature, and rejecting the natural as the ultimate end of human existence. The world has not caused our idolatry, rather our idolatry has wronged the world. St. Paul says it groans in the travails of childbirth until man and woman take up their abandoned post of cosmic priest again (Romans 8), and Kavanagh says we can only finally do the world the way it was meant to be done if we are restored to this liturgical relationship with the world. Sometimes the overly spiritual Christian suggests that redemption consists of turning a blind eye to the world, but in fact redemption consists of having our proper activity returned to us in *both* domains—the profane as well as the sacred. The pirate's patch ruins depth perception when placed over either eye, and when that happens both the spiritualist and the secularist see a flattened world, lacking its full dimension. The correction to our astigmatism consists of bringing spirit and matter into focus by a liturgical asceticism that enables an affirmation of images that sees the world as sacrament (the present chapter) and as sacrifice (the next chapter).

The third act of the drama is the recovery of lost memory. Christ never forgot his Father in Heaven, even while he was a man like us; and through baptismal incorporation he engraves (*sphragis*) his spiritual memory in us. We are therefore drawn to the place where we expect Jesus to pass by. Like the blind man in Mark 10, we take a position with the other catechumens near the place where we hear Jesus's disciples clamoring, and we shout, "Jesus, Son of David, have pity on me!" (Mark 10:46). If Jesus stops to ask what you want, answer you want to see (Mark 10:51). We are likewise drawn to a place near the pool of Siloam (John 9) so that if he tells us to go and wash, we can do so with alacrity. If we cannot answer for ourselves, let our parents express our desire for enlightenment when they are quizzed "What do you ask of God's Church?" Answer that we want the image of God to grow into a greater likeness of God. Because this healing is done by the Son of God, we receive more than we ask for. His grace exceeds our desire, and the measure of our request does not determine the measure by which God weighs out his gift. We had barely hoped to be admitted back into the Garden of Eden, and he would take us, like the bride in the Song of Songs, to the inner chambers of his own mansion in heaven. We had barely hoped to rejoin the serving staff, but he says, as he said concerning the prodigal son, "Quick! Bring the best baptismal robe and put it on him; put a filial ring on his finger; crucify the fatted lamb and prepare a eucharistic feast for him to eat."

If we are ever to appreciate God's grace, our hope must become more audacious than it is now. The new light that will emanate from our baptismal eye upon the world will be brighter than any light that could emanate from our created eye, because this will be the eye of the Dove. It is not our sight, improved; it is Christ's sight, infused. Our sight is now truly spiritual because the Holy Spirit, who arrived on the scene of Jesus's baptism to descend and alight on him in the form of the dove, arrives at our baptism to alight on us, too. For those of us who could not be there the first time, the Spirit of life hovers over the waters again, as he did in Genesis 1; for any of us who missed the flood in Genesis 6, God reenacts a personal flood to drown sins and rescue by ark; if we missed the escape from slavery in Exodus 14, or the sweet water at Marah, or the thirst-quenching water from the rock, or the Jordan's purification of Namaan, or the Jordan's parting for Joshua, or the invitation to repentance under the Forerunner's hand at the Jordan's banks, here in baptism they are all done for us again: our personal exodus, our personal quenching, our personal purification. All of salvation history runs downhill and pools in the baptismal font.

Paulinus of Nola combined water and light in his composition for the baptistery. "From this font," he writes, "which gives life to souls in need of salvation, flows a *living river of divine light*. The Holy Spirit comes down from heaven upon this river and joins the sacred waters with the heavenly source; the stream teems with God and from the eternal seed gives birth to holy offspring by its fruitful waters."[8] Bright water. Liquid light. A living river of divine light that plants a seed of holiness in us at baptism, which is membership in the mystical body of Christ, which is nourished by our liturgical life, which is strengthened by our liturgical asceticism, which bears fruit in our *diakonia* to the world, and which, at the ultimate heights, makes us also into light. Nicholas Cabasilas particularly emphasizes this eschatological dimension of baptism, when he says we cannot conclude then anything we do not begin now. So Cabasilas writes, "The life in Christ originates in this life and arises from it. It is perfected, however, in the life to come, when we shall have reached that last day. It cannot attain perfection in men's souls in this life, nor even in that which is to come, without already having begun

---

8. Paulinus of Nola, Letter 32, 5, cited in the General Audience of Pope John Paul II, April 12, 2000. http://rumkatkilise.org/byzpope.htm. Emphasis added.

here. . . . It is this life which is the workshop for all these things."[9] He offers an image of the baptized person as a fetus being formed for a life that it does not yet live completely. We can imagine the baby wondering why these bones are growing in length because it cannot use them in the restricted womb in which it finds itself, but one day it will know what to do with them. Likewise, we do not quite know what to do with the energies baptism has infused in us, but one day we will. And as this eschatological life forms in us, he concludes, "it is possible for the saints not only to be disposed and prepared for that life, but also even now to live and act in accordance with it."[10] This radiant life is what Ambrose saw illuminating his neophytes when they came forth clothed in white raiment, a soul pure and washed in the laver of regeneration. In the Song of Songs he hears Christ saying to the newly baptized: "Behold, thou art fair, My love, behold thou art fair, thy eyes are like a dove's," and Ambrose concludes that their "eyes are beautiful like those of a dove, because in the likeness of a dove the Holy Spirit descended from heaven."[11]

The saint is a deified person who does not merely reflect light, he becomes light. Evdokimov says the angels are a "second light," because they are messengers and servants, but man and woman's condition is different: they do not reflect light, as do the angels. "God gives to man, his image, the capacity to call forth the imperishable values of the matter of this world and to manifest holiness through his own body. In effect, man does not reflect light like the angels but becomes light."[12] The only begotten Son is the first bright one, whom Hebrews 1:3 says is "the radiance of God's glory," but then there are others plunged into the bright river that flows from him to be illuminated and enlightened, and bring spiritual light with them into the valley of the shadow of death. As Gregory Palamas said above, man's sight, when it is in action, now becomes light itself, and communes with the light, and sees with it.[13] Is it any

---

9. Nicholas Cabasilas, *The Life in Christ*, 43.

10. Ibid., 45.

11. Ambrose, *On the Mysteries*, chapter 7:37, *Nicene and Post-Nicene Fathers*, Vol. 10 (Peabody, MA: Hendrickson Publishers, Inc., 1999), 322.

12. Evdokimov, *The Art of the Icon*, 55–56.

13. Palamas, *Mary the Mother of God*, 48.

wonder that the least in the kingdom of heaven sees more to the world than do the greatest of those born only of women? (Luke 7:28). Ultraviolet light will show up what is hidden to ordinary light, and the saint's eyebeam will show up things hidden from the secular man. St. Francis saw a leper's body wanting an embrace; Mother Teresa saw a dying person as still precious; St. Lawrence saw gold as rubbish and the true treasures of the Church to be the poor and suffering. The eye of the Dove permits the Christian to see everything in a different light.

We become beautiful by coming close to God's Light and having such Light draw us upward. We might say that man and woman "fall upward" in this third act. It is a do-over of the Garden of Eden. The first Adam fell down in pride; when the second Adam came down it was not in pride but in a supreme act of humility, so his brothers and sisters could fall up. His *kenosis* elevates us (*prokope*). And the one of our race who has fallen furthest up is the purest one of our race, the Virgin Mary. She appeared on earth with a beauty that outshone the heavenly luminaries, becoming more honorable than the cherubim and more glorious beyond compare than the seraphim. When Psalm 45 says "the king's daughter is all glorious within her chamber," Gregory Palamas interpreted it to mean that Mary's glory is from within. "It pours forth like a light from within her to without, revealing to all those who see it the magnificence stored up inside her on account of her complete freedom from passion, and making known the nobility of her virginal soul."[14] Mary has the brightest eyebeam among the saints, because she is the most full of grace, and that means her tender gaze does not miss anything. She sees corners of the world, and little ones in it, that we would otherwise miss. She is the fountain of the Church's maternal care, and we are all in training to one day arrive at the place where Mary is already. She is a sign of the Church in its future glory "because what has been accomplished in her as a member surpassing all others will be accomplished in all the members of Christ's Mystical

14. Palamas, "On the Entry of the Mother of God into the Holy of Holies II," in *Mary the Mother of God*, 421.

Body."[15] We are developing over our lifetimes the grace that she possessed in fullness, so *Redemptoris Mater* says the path along which the Church journeys through time towards the consummation of the ages is simply the path already trodden by the Virgin Mary (¶2).

I know that we like to say the world is a sacrament, but I'm going to try to complexify this claim. I think we can only make it by including liturgical asceticism, the basis for mundane theology. A clear eye, newly restored, is required in order to see the world in a full sacramental light. This is because sacramentality is not an inherent state but a dynamic action. It is a verb. Let us approach this by placing sacrament within the genus of symbol, and begin by thinking about the operation of symbol.

The word's origin is from *sym* (together) and *ballein* (to throw). In ancient Greece, an object was broken in two, for example, a coin or a bone, to serve as a sign of mutual recognition in the future when the two pieces were "symbolized." Symbolizing is an action, a feat: the two halves are *thrown back together*. "To symbolize" does not mean performing an abstract mental act, or representing something to oneself, or substituting something for an absent reality; the coin is "symbolized" when its two parts are thrown together and create recognition. Regular symbols bring about a connection with regular things, and religious symbols throw us together with God. John Breck traces the religious symbol through four stages. First, it served as a simple sign of recognition by manifesting the presence of the sacred; second, it became the means of mutual participation, where *sumballein* meant a meeting or encounter between man and God; third, focus was turned to the material object itself, the *sumbolon*, that entered into contact with the realm of the sacred and communicated divine power to the realm of the profane; and fourth, all this was later applied to verbal expressions, e.g. consecratory formulas and incantations.[16]

15. Explanatory note before Mass of "The Blessed Virgin Mary, Queen of All Creation," *Collection of Masses of the Blessed Virgin Mary* (New York: Catholic Book Publishing Co., 1988), 43.

16. John Breck, *The Power of the Word* (Crestwood, NY: St. Vladimir's Seminary Press, 1986), 187.

By this understanding, we can conclude that a symbol that fails to symbolize is not a symbol. I mean this as more than a tautology: I mean it as an insight into what symbol accomplishes. If the object does not establish connection, does not throw two things together, does not affect both parties, then it is a failed symbol. Being a successful symbol requires that the span of the bridge touches both shores. There are three agents involved: the symbolizer, the symbol, and the recipient whom the symbol is supposed to unite with the giver. In addition to the symbolic object, we must consider the giver and the receiver of the symbol. Now shift the vocabulary from symbol back to sacrament. Saying that the world is sacrament is true as far as it goes: the cosmos certainly is a gift from Almighty God. But to be a true sacrament (a successful symbol), an encounter and connection must take place. Claiming that the world is sacramental is not merely a cosmological comment, it is a soteriological one, as well, which means that a complete theology of cosmic sacrament must attend not only to the symbol thrown, but to the symbolizer who throws it and the recipient who is required to catch it. If I may revert temporarily to the intromission theory of optics, the color blue does not exist in my pupil or in the light waves coming off the painting; the color blue *happens* when the light waves meet my pupil. Similarly, the sacrament does not exist in the world or in my mind, the sacrament *happens* when a cosmos successfully throws God and man together. In the sacraments, the world functions properly at last; it is Eden all over again; water and bread and wine and oil are the world being done rightly at last. The world itself is only one-third of the sacramental equation; that God is offering the world to us as sacramental symbol is another third; and our willingness to be thrown together with God by the world is the final third.

Liturgical asceticism makes its appearance in that final third, for it capacitates our receptivity. If the world is going to be sacrament for us, then liturgical asceticism is required because there is a power that opposes this symbolic potential of the world which must be overcome. The opposite of *symballein* is *diaballein*, which means to throw apart, and there is one with a diabolical will who strives to destroy the world's symbolic character. How will he (*el diablo*) be defeated? If we were so lucky that the problem was merely one of ignorance, then the world's sacramentality could be restored by some gnostic memo inviting us to contemplate the beauty of a sunrise and entertain thoughts of the transcendent. But the problem is more severe. It is not a problem of ignorance. Rather, it is a problem of will: our crippled will, to be exact, having come under attack by the devil. For the world to be sacrament, it is not enough to simply declare that it should be so. For the world to become sacramental again, Satan must be defeated, and his *pompa* opposed. And this only Christ can do, as Olivier Clément explains:

> In Christ the world is joined together again in symbol, in a profusion of symbols. The invisible part appears in the visible: the visible draws its meaning from the invisible. . . . God transcends the intelligible as well as the visible, but through the incarnation of the Logos he penetrates them both, transfigures and unites them. The world is a vast incarnation which the fall of the human race tries to contradict. The *diabolos*, the opposite of the *symbolon*, is continually trying to keep apart the separated halves of the ring; but they come together in Christ. Christian symbolism expresses nothing less than the union in Christ of the divine and the human —of which the cosmos becomes the dialogue—displaying the circulation in Christ of glory between "earth" and "heaven," between the visible and the invisible.[17]

The sacramentality of the world depends first upon Christ who is the primordial sacrament himself: he sym-bolizes (throws together) the human and divine in an alliance. Christ's hypostatic union is a verb, still in operation. Christ is the incarnate one who enters into contact with the realm of the profane in order to communicate divine power to it. He thereby restores the cosmos to function as sacramental dialogue. The world does not just sit there as a sacrament, it must be made to operate as a sacrament, and this only Christ can do because he has conquered Satan in fact. Now *consecration mundi* can occur. Now his victory can go and be transcribed, transferred, translated onto each of us personally, which liturgy does when it unites us to Christ's symbolic action because his lit-

---

17. Olivier Clément, *The Roots of Christian Mysticism*, 219.

urgy wields efficacious signs, called sacraments. The sacramentality of the world depends also upon the Church, which is a fundamental sacrament herself—her occupation is sym-bolizing, throwing together, reconnecting God and man, sacred and profane, heaven and earth, Uncreated and created, the Kingdom and this world. One of sin's consequences is that objects in the world no longer function sacramentally after we have been diabolically thrown apart from God, but the Church serves both God and mankind by re-sym-bolizing them.

The world of the liturgical person is completely different from the world of the idolater because for the liturgist the world has recovered its intended sacramentality. It is a different world he looks at. This is the foundation for mundane liturgical theology. The world can only finally function as sacrament if our hearts are ascetically capacitated for liturgy. Our eyes become capacitated for divine sights, and that includes the appearance of God amongst his creatures. Such an eyebeam discerns traces of the *Logos*-creator in the creature's *logoi*. Evagrius called the creatures "letters of the alphabet" making it possible for those far from God to come to knowledge of him. In his *Praktikos* he records an inquiry made to the hermit Anthony about how he gets along without the consolation of books, and Anthony replies, "My book, sir philosopher, is the nature of created things, and it is always at hand when I wish to read the words of God."[18] The cosmos is the first Bible, which always complements scripture because both books have the same author. The pre-Socratics understood the *logos* philosophically as the rational principle governing the cosmos. St. John the Evangelist, on the other hand, knew the *Logos* personally as the one who was in the beginning, was with God, who was God, and whose life was the light of all mankind. The world becomes theophany when it has been freed from the danger of idolatry, and becomes truly symbolic. Light meets light. The saint has a spiritual awareness of created objects because he or she sees the world in God's light with his eye of the Dove.

18. Evagrius Ponticus, *The Praktikos & Chapters on Prayer* (Kalamazoo: Cistercian Publications, 1981), 39.

The affirmation of images will require both creation and redemption to work synergistically. Redemption is not plan B, to be put into effect after plan A has failed. God did not discard creation in favor of an alternate one. This is why *consecratio mundi* is *not* the removal of a thing from the profane (more on that in the next chapter). When John exercised his eyebeams on the island of Patmos and saw a new heavens, a new earth, and a new humanity, he was not seeing a replacement but, rather, a perfection. Redemption lets creation operate correctly, finally. Why did God put two rational, embodied creatures in the midst of a material world instead of just creating more angels? Gregory Palamas offers his answer: "The reason mankind was brought into being by God was so that they might apprehend with their senses the sky, the earth, and everything they contain, as visible objects, and by means of them go beyond them with their minds to invisible beauties, that they might sing the praises of God, the one Creator of all."[19]

Adam and Eve were placed in the Garden of Symbols so that every created thing could point to its Creator; we, their children, are made for the affirmation of images, which point beyond themselves to invisible beauties. Liturgy's splendid beauty elevates matter to its real dignity and final destiny because it tells the truth about the world's source and end. The transfiguration experienced at every liturgy is thereafter the light by which we see every creature transfigured—including the creature of time: thus the liturgy of the hours and the liturgical year. Time was created by God, and as one of his creatures it obeys him. We are the ones who have a problem with time, because, to the sinner who suffers a sickness unto death, time looks like sand through an hourglass or a wheel of deadly fortune. We feel its repetitive cycles as proof of meaninglessness. But to the liturgist with an eschatological eyebeam, the rising and falling of successive days, weeks, or years are like the rising and falling of waves that steadily push a piece of driftwood closer to the shore, where Christ waits for us. Thus the Divine Liturgy, the liturgy of the hours, the sacraments and sacramentals, and our personal liturgies of devotion, piety, and ministry to charity are all symbolical points

19. Palamas, *Mary the Mother of God*, 421.

at which the reign of God reaches across the divide that diabolical sin has constructed.

The world will fulfill its sacramental function in us when the disorder inherited from the first Adam is cured by the second Adam. Egocentrism ruined theocentrism, and this has had a fallout on cosmology. But the Incarnation restored theocentrism, and this has had cosmological fallout of enabling us to finally do the world the way the world was meant to be done, namely, as sacrament and sacrifice. We deliver the world when we ourselves are delivered from worldliness. In his famous essay, "The Weight of Glory," C. S. Lewis summarizes his romantic theology by saying that things in the world only tease us toward something greater:

> The books or the music in which we thought the beauty was located will betray us if we trust to them; it is not in them, it only came through them, and what came through them was longing. . . . For they are not the thing itself; they are only the scent of a flower we have not found, the echo of a tune we have not heard, news from a country we have never yet visited. Do you think I am trying to weave a spell? Perhaps I am; but remember your fairy tales. Spells are used for breaking enchantments as well as for inducing them. And you and I have need of the strongest spell that can be found to wake us from the evil enchantment of worldliness which has been laid upon us for nearly a hundred years. Almost our whole education has been directed to silencing this shy, persistent, inner voice; almost all our modern philosophies have been devised to convince us that the good of man is to be found on this earth.[20]

Tolkien broke that spell of worldliness in Lewis one night in 1931, when they had a long conversation while strolling down Addison's Walk. Afterward, Tolkien went home and wrote a poem about the discussion. He titled it *Mythopoeia* and dedicated it to Lewis: "To one who said that myths were lies and therefore worthless, even though 'breathed through silver.'" Its opening lines describe the outlook of a worldly materialist:

---

20. C. S. Lewis, "The Weight of Glory" essay in *The Weight of Glory* (San Francisco: HarperCollins, 2001), 31.

A star's a star, some matter in a ball
compelled to courses mathematical
amid the regimented, cold, inane,
where destined atoms are each moment slain.[21]

That outlook (eyebeam) is very dim. It sees a world of dead matter; sees no *logoi* within it, and no *Logos* behind it; no sacramentality is possible in such a mechanical, solipsistic universe. And Lewis learned his lesson. He repeats Tolkien's thesis but puts it on the lips of a retired star named Ramandu in *Voyage of the Dawn Treader*:

"Every morning a bird brings me a fire-berry from the valleys in the Sun, and each fire-berry takes away a little of my age. And when I have become as young as the child that was born yesterday, then I shall take my rising again (for we are at earth's eastern rim) and once more tread the great dance."

"In our world," said Eustace, "a star is a huge ball of flaming gas."

"Even in your world, my son, that is not what a star is but only what it is made of."[22]

Natural science looks at what a thing is made of, but there is something that *stands under* the highest magnification setting on the microscope, and that is what theological science looks at. Theology looks at the *sub-stance* of things, and in its sub-stance, the world is sacramental. Mrs. Murphy is a theologian insofar as she can see that substance. Mrs. Murphy is a cosmic priest insofar as she can put creation's glorification into words: liturgical words, words of praise. Mrs. Murphy is an ascetic insofar as she is able to accomplish this. Mrs. Murphy is a mundane liturgical theologian insofar as she undims her spiritual eye to see the world properly. If we content ourselves with only seeing what the thing is made of, then we never go beyond the thing, and we will never become the persons we were created in the beginning to be. Worldliness is the snake eating his

21. J.R.R. Tolkien, *Tree and Leaf: Including "Mythopoeia"* (New York: Harper-Collins, 2001).

22. C.S. Lewis, *Voyage of the Dawn Treader*, in *The Chronicles of Narnia*, collected edition (San Francisco: HarperCollins, 2001), 522.

own tail, but sacramentality is every creature pointedly glorifying its Creator.

So the liturgist makes his journey with regularity, twice crossing a threshold, once in each direction. First he crosses the narthex from the world into the nave, in order to absorb the energy of the altar in the sanctuary; then he crosses the narthex from the nave back into the world, in order to release that light into the world. Phosphorescence, I read, is a process by which the energy absorbed by a substance is slowly released in the form of light. Exactly! We absorb the energy of Mount Tabor at every liturgy, we ingest the substance of Christ at the Eucharist, and by the light this releases in us we see the world liturgically. This explains the coexistence and interaction of sacred with profane. People ask why we need the sacred seven sacraments if the profane world is a sacrament. The answer is, we come in for eye surgery. We cannot return to our place in the cosmic liturgy until our priesthood has been repaired. The ordained priesthood sacramentally equips the common priesthood for its mundane cosmic priesthood. The man in the sanctuary ministers to the men and women in the nave so they can resume beyond the narthex the liturgical career that Adam and Eve had forfeited.

5

The Voice of the Dove

I HAVE BEEN PROPOSING a connection between liturgy and life, such that what we do outwardly in liturgy expresses what we are becoming inwardly, and that inward identity is an ongoing conversion that does the world differently. We do the world sacramentally (last chapter) and sacrificially (this chapter). Interestingly enough, and contrary to a faulty understanding of sacrifice that many carry around with them, the sacrificial dimension of the world will be better explained by the affirmation of images than by their negation. Williams said Athanasius described the Incarnation as an act that took Manhood into God. The taking up of Mankind is simultaneously an affirmation of images and a sacrificial gesture. Christ descends to his people in order to lift us and our world into his way of life. His is the way of joyful sacrifice. How is this done?

Archimedes was a Greek physicist and inventor who was fascinated with the mathematics of the lever. A quick review of what I learned in junior high science about simple machines reminds me that a lever is used to exert a large force over a small distance, by exerting a small force over a greater distance at the other end of the lever. A child can thus with one hand lift a man standing on the short end of the beam if the child presses down on the long end of the beam. Archimedes was so fascinated by the lever's potential that one day he famously exclaimed "Give me a lever and a place to stand, and I shall move the Earth." He realized he needed three things in order to move the earth: a long enough lever, a correctly placed fulcrum point, and a place to stand. Of course, that last requirement was the problem. How could he apply leverage to the world when he, himself, was standing upon the world? How could he step off the thing he lives on in order to move it? He had no footing. So in philosophy this riddle became known as searching for the "Archimedean point," i.e., an objective standpoint removed from the object of study. This hypothetical point of perspective is thought to be far enough removed from something as to afford an outsider's view of it. But how can we remove ourselves to a point outside ourselves?

I offer you Archimedes's puzzle not as case of physics or philosophy, but as a spiritual metaphor. Augustine defined sin as *incurvatus in se*—being curved in upon oneself; a life oriented inwardly toward self, rather than outwardly toward God and others. Our egocentrism exerts so strong a gravitational pull that it bends the light of glory back upon ourselves that should be glorifying God. How can we move ourselves off-center when we are the center of our own universe? We have no leverage over sin. We have no standpoint outside our vanity and pride. We have no rock on which to stand that is beyond our self-interest. Whoever desires to get outside of himself needs some sort of Archimedean point beyond himself. And I want to propose that this is precisely what the liturgy offers us: the lever is the wood of the cross; the fulcrum is the altar; and the firm spot on which to stand—the Archimedean point which is in the world but not of it—is the rock of Peter, the Church. The liturgy performed there moves the world. Liturgy is not celebrated to ignore the world, it is celebrated to lift the world. It gives us a lever and a place on which to stand, so that we can elevate the world toward the heavenly Jerusalem. By "elevation" I mean sacrifice. I'm talking about lifting up our ordinary, daily, mundane life in sacrifice to God. This sacrificial life sings with the voice of the Dove.

Mundane liturgical theology is curious about the spiritual mathematics of this liturgical lever. Its attention, therefore, expands beyond the Church sanctuary, where the liturgy is celebrated in sacrament and ceremony, to the world outside, where the liturgy is done in life. The sacramental liturgy and our personal liturgy are connected. We see again why Kavanagh defined liturgy as doing the world the way the world was meant to be done. When the liturgy is put in motion, it further moves the world. The liturgy does not simply move within the sacred sphere, it has consequential movement within the profane sphere. Understanding this will require a refreshed understanding of the relationship between the sacred and the profane, the very understanding helped by the affirmation of images. Recall again what Paul VI said about *consecratio mundi.* It does *not* mean "the separation of a thing from what is profane in order to reserve it exclusively, or particularly, for the Divinity."[1] It *does* mean "the re-establishment of a thing's relationship to God according to its own order, according to the exigency of the nature of the thing itself, in the plan willed by God."[2]

Untold mischief has been done by an equivocation over that word "profane." More often than not, we use it pejoratively, as if it describes something in opposition to God. It drags in its wake other words, which a quick glance at a thesaurus identifies as "desecrated, vulgar, obscene, uncouth, offensive, sacrilegious, and impure." If that's what we think profane means, no wonder some think the best strategy is to avoid it altogether. Because the profane concerns the world, we think it means worldly, in the sinful sense. But that is not the origin of the word. The temple the priest went into was called the *fanum,* and the *pro-fanum* referred to the area outside the temple gates. The profane is not an antithesis to God, but simply an antithesis to the sacred. "Sacred" means fenced off or set apart; "profane" means not set apart, the surroundings outside the fence. To be sacred means to be set aside for special activity; profane means ordinary activity, it does not mean impure activity. Thomas Aquinas said "Something is called sacred, *sacrum*, because of its relation to the act of public worship, *ad cultum divinum*,"[3] and only in relation to the sacred action are persons, places, times, etc. called sacred. But this does not imply that the profane is godless or unholy. The existence of the sacred does not mean that God is only present in the sanctuary and not in the world. The relationship between sacred and profane is an itinerant relationship: it involves going in and coming out. Sacred and profane exist in a liminal relationship,

---

1. Paul VI, "Layman Should Be World's Perfect Citizen."

2. Ibid.

3. Thomas Aquinas, *Summa Theologica* 2-2, 99, 1. Cited in the very helpful chapter on sacred and profane by Joseph Pieper, *In Search of the Sacred* (San Francisco: Ignatius Press, 1991), 25.

but the boundary we are talking about is one that fences off a place where we can be sure to find God waiting, it does not fence God off from his own world, the very one he created and supports.

The sacred and the profane need each other, each for its own completion. The liturgical life into which we are baptized unfolds across both spheres.[4] The sacred priesthood is practiced in the sanctuary, the profane priesthood is practiced in the secular world, and *Lumen Gentium* ¶34 states that the laity is involved in both. They exercise their priesthood on both ends of the liturgical lever. The common priesthood of the laity assists at the sacred Mass and is active in the mundane world:

> For this reason the laity, dedicated to Christ and anointed by the Holy Spirit, are marvelously called and wonderfully prepared so that ever more abundant fruits of the Spirit may be produced in them. For all their works, prayers and apostolic endeavors, their ordinary married and family life, their daily occupations, their physical and mental relaxation, if carried out in the Spirit, and even the hardships of life, if patiently borne—all these become "spiritual sacrifices acceptable to God through Jesus Christ" (1 Pt. 2:5). Together with the offering of the Lord's body, they are most fittingly offered in the celebration of the Eucharist. Thus, as those everywhere who adore in holy activity, the *laity consecrate the world itself to God*.[5]

Our entire daily life, excepting nothing, can become a spiritual sacrifice acceptable to God through the supreme and eternal priest, Jesus Christ, who vivifies his mystical members' lives in his Spirit and gives them a share in his spiritual worship, conducted for the glory of God and the salvation of humankind. By operating the leverage of the cross we consecrate the entire world (*consecratio mundi*), and all our daily actions, to God.

The Christian can therefore be said to participate in two liturgies: what Jean Corbon called the celebrated liturgy and the lived

---

4. Kavanagh would say in class that God works on both sides of the Church-world equation.

5. *Lumen Gentium* ¶34. Emphasis added.

liturgy,[6] or what Ion Bria called the liturgy, and the liturgy after the liturgy.[7] The sacred is the sanctuary/nave; the profane is the world; and the narthex is the membrane between them which the Christian crosses in a dialectical rhythm on a regular basis. We cross it when we go to assist at the sacrifice of the Mass, bringing along with us what we have gathered throughout the week in order to place everything at the foot of the altar. And we cross it again when we obey the presider's command *Ite, missa est*, bringing along with us the graces we have received in the mysteries in order to place ourselves at the service of charity. Liturgies start and stop, the liturgy does not. The liturgy that Christ celebrates in eternity has no ending or pause, and neither should our liturgical life. It would not be good for a heart to be stopped and restarted on a regular basis: a fibrillating liturgy also puts the Christian in peril. It would not be good for a lung to only inhale: a liturgy that does not exhale the fragrance of Christ when it leaves the Church would asphyxiate Christians. The sacred liturgy ought not be secreted in a parallel universe that has no effect on our profane life. Mundane liturgical theology puts its attention on how the world beyond the narthex is moved by this liturgy.

Within the sacred, the altar serves as a table of the Lord, Golgotha in stone, and, on behalf of the profane sphere, a fulcrum which balances the cross as it leverages the world's elevation. Recall all that we have said so far: that in Ephesians Paul describes the entire reason for creation, Israel's salvation history, and the Paschal mystery as a mysterious effort on God's part to bring mankind to heaven and into union with him; that the Church Fathers repeatedly said God became human so that human beings might be made divine; that Chrysostom summarized the mystery in eight words: God would have man seated up on high; that the Logos descended (*kenosis*) in order to elevate humanity (*prokope*).The Incarnation was not so much the conversion of Godhead into flesh, but the taking of Manhood into God. The raising of humankind to fellowship with God is the aim of both creation and salvation history, and it is the aim that

6. Corbon, *The Wellspring of Worship*.
7. Bria, *The Liturgy after the Liturgy*.

liturgy serves. Give me the Church as a foundation on which to stand, and the beam of the cross to work under my daily world like a prybar, and when the weight of heaven descends on the sacred end of the liturgical lever, my world on the other end will be elevated.

What shall we call this elevation? What name shall we give to this ascending activity? I will call it *sacrifice*, aware that the word will need to be defended. As much damage has been done by a faulty concept of sacrifice as has been done by a faulty concept of the profane. In our modern grammar, sacrifice is usually associated with a bitter meaning. It has come to mean giving up something; therefore, it is accompanied by sadness and regret; and therefore we prefer to keep it as small as possible. But the *Catechism of the Catholic Church* places sacrifice in the very different grammar of giving something to someone: therefore, it is accompanied by a joy that issues from the happiness we feel at the happiness of the one who receives it; and therefore we prefer to make it as large as possible. Thomas Aquinas treats religion in the part of his *Summa* that deals with the cardinal virtues of prudence, justice, fortitude, and temperance. Specifically, he treats religion in the section dealing with justice, because justice means giving another what he is due. And what is God due? The virtue of religion. "Charity leads us to render to God what we as creatures owe him in all justice," says the Catechism in paragraph 2095, and then succeeding paragraphs identify the ingredients of this virtue, punctuated by subheadings that I include among these partial quotations:

Adoration

2096: "adoration is the first act of the virtue of religion" and it involves acknowledging God as Creator and humbling oneself in submission.

2097: "the worship of the one God sets man free from turning in on himself, from the slavery of sin and the idolatry of the world."

Prayer

2098: "lifting up the mind toward God is an expression of our adoration of God: prayer of praise and thanksgiving, intercession and petition."

Sacrifice

2099: "it is right to offer sacrifice to God as a sign of adoration and gratitude, supplication and communion. 'Every action done so as to cling to God in communion of holiness, and thus achieve blessedness, is a true sacrifice.'"

That closing definition of sacrifice comes from St. Augustine. Sacrifice is clinging to God, communion of holiness, achieving blessedness. Should such a posture cause regret? Is blessedness bitter?

When the world is done correctly (righteously) in liturgy, then the world's sacrificial composition becomes clear. Its cosmic harmony is composed as a song of glory to its Creator, to whom it wants to pour itself out. But mute matter needs a voice. Electrons and solar systems glorify God by obeying his laws over their nature, but they do not glorify God reasonably, with reason, with word, with *logos*, with *logike latreia* (Romans 12:1). That would require creatures created in the image of the Logos, who is the image of God. So cosmic priests were added. Gregory of Nazianzus calls them microcosms—hybrids—for being both spirit and body, and thus able to offer up the sacrifice of material creation: "In some way a new universe was born, small and great at one and the same time. God set this hybrid worshiper on earth to contemplate the visible world, and to be initiated into the invisible; to reign over earth's creatures, and to obey orders from on high."[8] Men and women are the tongue of creation's sacrificial praise to its Creator. They are enrolled simultaneously as citizens in both the invisible and visible realms, both the empyrean and the empirical. Schmemann calls them *homo adorans*—a creature who adores:

> All rational, spiritual and other qualities of man, distinguishing him from other creatures, have their focus and ultimate fulfillment in this capacity to bless God, to know, so to speak, the meaning of the thirst and hunger that constitutes his life. "*Homo sapiens,*" "*homo faber*" . . . yes, but, first of all, "*homo adorans.*" The first, the basic definition of man is that he is *the priest*. He stands

in the center of the world and unifies it in his act of blessing God, of both receiving the world from God and offering it to God—and by filling the world with this eucharist, he transforms his life, the one that he receives from the world, into life in God, into communion with Him. The world was created as the "matter," the material of one all-embracing eucharist, and man was created as the priest of this cosmic sacrament.[9]

The fall was the forfeiture of our liturgical career, baptism is its resumption, and liturgical asceticism is our gymnasium for training in our renewed life. The Fall silenced the eucharistic, sacrificial hymn intended for our lips, but Christ restored it when he joined us, became a second Adam, and sang it to his Father through human throat. He is now giving the voice of the Dove to each one of us so we may continue to add new notes to the hymn. By sacramental grace, our ability to conduct a sacrificial world is renewed.

The liturgical altar thus becomes the fulcrum upon which the wood of the cross can make our world new and lift it sacrificially to God. Emile Mersch defines sacrifice as "the supreme act of religion," and then defines religion as "a conscious and deliberate straining of the creature toward the Creator, an aspiration toward God, a desire of nearness and union with Him, as far as this is possible for a creature."[10] Under this definition, the Son does a more perfect religion than ours. His desire for nearness and union with the Father is far more intense than ours, his straining and aspiration more committed than ours; and yet, as far as it is possible in creatures like ourselves, the Holy Spirit brings about the same in us. Jesus creates true religion in us by spiritually cloning his own sacrificial posture towards God in us. The liturgy is not the performance of a human religion; liturgy is the religion of Christ perpetuated in Christians. Sacrifice is the supreme act of religion, and Christ sustained this state over every moment because his entire life was a sacrifice as he forever aspired toward God his Father in true religion. Religion is

9. Alexander Schmemann, *For the Life of the World* (Crestwood, NY: St. Vladimir's Seminary Press, 1973), 15.

10. Mersch, *Theology of the Mystical Body,* 580.

an appetite for God that is expressed by sacrifice, as Schmemann articulates:

> Bread and wine. By bringing these humble human gifts—our earthly food and drink—and placing them on the altar, we perform, often without thinking of it, that most ancient, primordial rite that from the first day of human history constituted the core of every religion: we offer a sacrifice to God.... From the time of Cain and Abel the blood of sacrifices has daily covered the earth and the smoke of burnt offerings has unceasingly risen to heaven.
>
> Our "refined" sensibilities are horrified by these blood sacrifices, by these "primitive" religions. In our horror, however, do we not forget and lose something very basic, very primary, without which in essence there is no religion? For in its ultimate depths religion is nothing other than *thirst for God....* In the sacrifice man gives himself and his own over to his God, because, knowing God, he cannot but love him, and loving him, he cannot but strive toward him and toward unity with him.[11]

An appetite is any tendency of a thing toward the good that fulfills it. Our bodies have an appetite for food because they need bread in order to live. But man does not live by bread alone. We also have souls whose appetite is for fellowship with God, the final good toward whom we tend because only he can finally satisfy us. The doctrine of original sin simply says that our appetite for God was spoiled after Adam and Eve ate a kind of knowledge before they were ready for it, and if our appetite for God would be restored, it must be trained in a new diet, a eucharistic diet. Christ was hungry for God, and God alone, and when we eat his body, he gives us his appetite. His entire life was one of sacrifice to the Father, and he places this perfect sacrifice in the hands of his Church not only so that she can offer it in the sanctuary, but also so that Christian lives can be ringed with religion. We can cling to God at every moment.

Lumen Gentium describes our Christian life of sacrifice by means of a patchwork of Scripture passages gathered together in paragraph

---

11. Alexander Schmemann, *The Eucharist* (Crestwood, NY: St. Vladimir's Seminary Press, 1988), 101–02.

10.[12] Christ is the great High Priest (Hebrews 5) who has made a new people consisting of two new identities: first, they are a kingdom and second, they are priests (Revelation 6). A kingdom is the realm where a king rules, and in this case God rules our heart and will; a priest is one who makes sacrifices, and in this case the sacrifices are spiritual and offered through all the works done by the Christian man and woman (1 Peter 2). We have been made into a spiritual house and a holy priesthood by regeneration and anointing by the Holy Spirit in order to be presented as a living sacrifice, holy and pleasing to God (Romans 12). Thus the world becomes a sacrament of communion, and our hearts become sacrificial altars on which every truth, beauty, and goodness the world has can be offered up to God.

Clinging to God is a sacrificial posture, but ever since we left the Garden of Eden we have been living in such an unnatural, crippled posture that we are surprised by it. We do not do nature naturally anymore, giving sacrifice a bad reputation. Letting loose of our grip on things is the preliminary act required of us before we can offer up any holy oblation in peace, and that discomfort is usually all we notice, the way a child can't get his attention past the shot he is going to receive at the doctor's office, even though there is health and glory on the backside. If I am a lover of self from self-interest, then surrendering that self will come with a certain amount of discomfort. Prying loose that self-interest will produce a certain amount of friction. The old Adam will ask *"What do I have to sacrifice?"* meaning, what am I required to give up? What is expected of me, which I must begrudgingly surrender if I want God to leave me

12. The text of *Lumen Gentium* ¶10 reads: "Christ the Lord, High Priest taken from among men, made the new people 'a kingdom and priests to God the Father.' The baptized, by regeneration and the anointing of the Holy Spirit, are consecrated as a spiritual house and a holy priesthood, in order that through all those works which are those of the Christian man they may offer spiritual sacrifices and proclaim the power of Him who has called them out of darkness into His marvelous light. Therefore all the disciples of Christ, persevering in prayer and praising God, should present themselves as a living sacrifice, holy and pleasing to God. Everywhere on earth they must bear witness to Christ and give an answer to those who seek an account of that hope of eternal life which is in them."

alone? That is Adam and Eve speaking from the bushes where they have hidden themselves from God, and the human race will never be able to develop a true theology of sacrifice from that locality. But the new Adam will ask *"What do I have to sacrifice?"* meaning, what do I possess that I may offer up to his glory? What do I have that I could sacrifice in order to please God and cling to him?

How do we make this transition? How do we strip off the old Adam to join in the sacrificial joy of the new Adam, who did not begrudge anything to his Father in heaven and wished only for his Father's glory? It seems impossible, but God has made it possible, which is precisely the gospel we preach. At one point in our frail history, the second of those persons of the Trinity was sent by the first of those persons of the Trinity, to be made man in the womb of the Virgin Mary by the third of those persons of the Trinity. They did so in order to transform us. What Christ is by nature, we are to become by grace. For him, this felt natural; for us, the straightening of bent bones in the splint will feel uncomfortable. But it can be done. The pinch bar of the cross can pry our ego out of our own hands, pry our world out of our own will, and then Christ can invite us to assist at his own liturgical cult. Asceticism will capacitate us for liturgy. At the ascension he sent the Spirit and now the Dove's voice joins ours in a kind of throat singing (overtone chanting).

The beginning of this life is called repentance, which Greek speakers called *metanoia*, from *meta* (beyond, above) and *nous* (mind). To repent is to receive a new mind. Have this mind among yourselves, which is yours in Christ Jesus for whom sacrificial love was such a delight that even though he had equality with God, he did not grasp at it. Then we will be re-trained in the virtue of religion under the tutelage of our Divine Pedagogue, and all the things in the world will lead us to God. Everything will be seen to be raw material for the sacrifice that humanity was commissioned to make of the world. The Lamb of God takes away the sins of the world, we sing at Mass, by making the world sacrificial. The affirmation of images will rise out of a sacrificial world which knows the spiritual way of the Dove. The material we have been given in order to make sacrifice is fine. It is not a problem. The dualist philosophers were wrong in supposing there is a problem with matter or bodies. They were wrong because the fall was spiritual, not material, which will only be righted by a spiritual rebirth that gives revival to sacrifice. Liturgy is doing with the world what was meant to be done with it.

How we managed to make the world worldly is the mystery of iniquity: somehow we took a gift from God that is thoroughly good and used it for sin. How the world is made sacrifice again is the mystery of salvation: somehow God re-trains our priestly hands so that they will operate the world eucharistically again. This requires regular exposure to the light of Mount Tabor that will illuminate everything with a different brightness, which is why we return again and again to the liturgy. Into the updraft of the liturgy we place our desires, affections, intentions, hopes, values, and loves so that they will be carried to heaven and purified in the refiner's fire, the Holy Spirit who lit the bush before Moses, settled in glory upon the tabernacle, overshadowed the Virgin Mary, and rested upon the twelve disciples to make them apostles of the resurrection. Worldliness is when the world is not brought to the sacred altar for oblation; but worldliness is overcome when we set the world upon its trajectory toward the eternal. Liturgical sacrifice reestablishes matter in the eucharistic hierarchy: God's love descends, and creation's thanksgiving ascends. Christian liturgists can use anything and everything from the mundane world as material for their spiritual sacrifices. A Christian liturgist who is pure in heart can affirm all images from the secular world.

The Church is sent to continue the redemptive work of Jesus Christ, which will involve the renewal of the whole temporal order. This work includes the ordained priest and the vowed religious, but the profane belongs to the laity in a special way because they are members of the caravan that crosses the narthex boundary between world and nave weekly, or daily, a company of pilgrims organized and equipped for this regular journey. (There is special opportunity for a theology of the permanent diaconate at this point, since the Deacon has been called "a cleric living a lay life"[13] and his ministry finds him both at the altar and in the midst of the secular with the

---

13. It is James Keating's observation. See *The Heart of the Diaconate: Communion with the Servant Mysteries of Christ* (New York: Paulist Press, 2015), 57.

lay baptized. He is a bilocating man who rides the river of liturgy from the altar to the street outside where he serves by rubbing shoulders with the People of God in their secular life.)

The residue of our defective definition of profane threatens to confuse us again. We think of passages in the Old Testament where the prophet seems to square off against the priest. Isaiah overhears the Lord to say, "What do I care for the multitude of your sacrifices? . . . In the blood of calves, lambs, and goats I find no pleasure" (Isaiah 1:11). Or Psalm 40 asserts, "Sacrifice and offering you do not want. . . . Holocaust and sin-offering you do not request," and the book of Hebrews quotes this passage as if it appears on the lips of Christ when he came into the world.[14] But we should not misunderstand these passages to mean the prophet opposes the priest's practice of the sacred cult. The prophet does not mind someone going into the temple—he is only bothered if a person does not take the temple with him when he comes back out! The prophet is not criticizing the practice of cultic religion, though he is criticizing the fact that what has been tilled in the sacred cult (cultivated) does not produce seed that takes root in the daily world. This should put an end to the baseless antagonism between liturgists and social justice ministries. We do not go into liturgy in order to escape the world, we go there to learn how to do it the correct way, so that we can come out inspired with righteousness. We go into liturgy to learn the song of holiness so as to sing it more bravely. The life of sacrifice is a life of service, morality, justice, ethics, and done joyfully, not begrudgingly.

Three official documents of the Church outline this job description of the laity in a special way. First, *Lumen Gentium* 31 says

What specifically characterizes the laity is their secular nature. . . . [T]he laity, by their very vocation, seek the kingdom of God by

14. Hebrews 10:5–7. "Therefore, when Christ came into the world, he said:
   'Sacrifice and offering you did not desire,
   but a body you prepared for me;
   with burnt offerings and sin offerings
   you were not pleased.'
   Then I said, 'Here I am—it is written about me in the scroll—
   I have come to do your will, my God.'"

engaging in temporal affairs and by ordering them according to the plan of God. They live in the world, that is, in each and in all of the secular professions and occupations. They live in the ordinary circumstances of family and social life, from which the very web of their existence is woven. They are called there by God that by exercising their proper function and led by the spirit of the Gospel they may work for the sanctification of the world from within as a leaven.[15]

Question: where shall I go to seek the kingdom of God? Answer: engage in temporal affairs and order them according to the plan of God. The mission and nature of the Church is realized in a special way by lay members whose field of operation is the profane. Karl Rahner defines a layperson as someone who has a *place-in-the-world*: "The layman is originally in the world in virtue of the *pre*-Christian position of his existence; in *this* place, and not in any other, is he to be a Christian. This he must be, not just 'in addition', but by christianizing his original pre-Christian situation . . . in such a way that precisely where there is the world and not the Church, the kingdom of God may begin to exist through him as a member of the Church."[16] In contrast to a monk who leaves the world for the monastery, and in contrast to an ordained priest who obediently goes wherever his bishop sends him, the laity retain their place, and retain it *as a Christian*. Rahner seems to be saying that the lay Christian has a mission, but the lay Christian's mission is not to go anywhere. The laity are not "sent out," and yet somehow we are to say that the laity have an apostolate. They face the same routine, the same neighbor, the same world-place, but with a different countenance. In this mission, the person does not change places, rather the person changes the place by making the world whole by means of a sacrificial affirmation of ordinary life. The laity remain precisely where they are, and christianize this marriage, this family, this job, this suburban cul-de-sac.

This is exactly how our second document describes things. The

15. *Lumen Gentium* ¶31.
16. Karl Rahner, "Notes on the Lay Apostolate," *Theological Investigations*, Vol. 2 (New York: Seabury Press, 1975), 323.

Decree on the Apostolate of the Laity (*Apostolicam Actuositatem*) says "In fulfilling this mission of the Church, the Christian laity exercise their apostolate *both in the Church and in the world*, in both the spiritual and the temporal orders. These orders, although distinct, are so connected in the singular plan of God that He Himself intends to raise up the whole world again in Christ and to make it a new creation, initially on earth and completely on the last day."[17] The laity have an apostolate in both the sacred and profane because both realms are connected in God's singular plan, and the new creation is raised up and comes out of their interaction. The sacred transfigures the profane, like yeast transfigures dough, and the profane result is a nourishing loaf. The world is kept from becoming worldly by its consecration, which orientates it by a sacred north star that rises over the entire profane horizon. This will not be completed until the last day, but it has already begun, and members of Christ's body, the Church, are given an apostolate in both spheres so that they can leverage the world's transfiguration. In their holiness, the laity "[conform] their lives to their faith so that they become the light of the world and attract all to the love of the true and good, and finally to the Church and to Christ."[18]

Third, an Apostolic Exhortation published in 1988 after the World Synod of Bishops, titled *Christifideles Laici*, says the profane is the locale for the laity's participation "in the threefold mission of Christ as Priest, Prophet and King."[19] Responsibilities in each of those missions are identified. First, the lay faithful share in the *priestly* mission of Jesus because "incorporated in Jesus Christ, the baptized are united to him and to his sacrifice in the offering they make of themselves and their daily activities." Second, through the laity's participation in the *prophetic* mission of Christ they are "given the ability and responsibility to accept the gospel in faith and to proclaim it in word and deed. . . . [They] are also called to allow the numinous and the power of the gospel to shine out every day in

---

17. *Apostolicam Actuositatem*, 5 (emphasis added).
18. Ibid., 13.
19. *Christifideles Laici* ¶14. The remaining quotations in this paragraph come from that source.

their family and social life." In the framework of their secular life they should express their hope of future glory, even in the midst of the contradictions of the present age. Third, the lay faithful "exercise their *kingship* as Christians" in two particular ways: "above all in the spiritual combat in which they seek to overcome in themselves the kingdom of sin, and then to make a gift of themselves so as to serve, in justice and in charity, Jesus who is himself present in all his brothers and sisters, above all in the very least." This kingship particularly seeks to "restore to creation all its original value" by "ordering it to the authentic well-being of humanity in an activity governed by the life of grace."

There is plenty to do in the world if we are to live it sacrificially and sing it with the voice of the Dove to the glory of God. Christ is prophet, priest, and king; he is the truth, the life, and the way. And every Christian (ordained and lay, sacred and secular) participates in those three offices, though in different modes. All are united to Christ's sacrifice in their self-offering, in splendoring the hope of future glory, in overcoming the kingdom of sin and making of themselves a gift to God. These are sacrificial modalities which do not take a Christian out of the world, but rather transform the world the Christian is in. So when Pope Paul VI said the Church "has an authentic secular dimension, inherent to her inner nature and mission,"[20] *Christifideles Laici* concludes from it that "The Church, in fact, *lives in the world, even if she is not of the world* (John 17:16). She is sent to continue the redemptive work of Jesus Christ, which 'by its very nature concerns the salvation of humanity, and also involves the renewal of the whole temporal order.'"[21]

We have found it, at last! The Archimedean point for which we were searching appears at last. On the one hand, we cannot lift up the world in sacrificial praise so long as we place our footing on the world alone; it is like trying to lift the carpeting while we stand on it. But on the other hand, where can we find a different footing in

---

20. Paul VI, Talk to Members of Secular Institutes (February 2, 1972): AAS 64 (1972), 208.

21. *Christifideles Laici*, ¶15 (emphasis added).

the world? Archimedes's problem was applying leverage to a world that he could not step off of in order to move it. But we can. Baptism has freed us from the world and simultaneously slipped under our standing the foundation we need to transfigure the world. The Church is in the world, but not of it. Precisely. We leave the world in order to bless the kingdom of God, and we do so for the sake of the world. This accounts for Christians' ambivalent attitude towards the world, both loving it and being indifferent to it. There is both an affirmation and negation of the images in the world. Josemaría Escrivá says, "All the things of the world are no more than dirt," but he immediately concludes the entry by adding "Place them in a heap under your feet and you'll be so much nearer to heaven."[22] Elsewhere he adds, "The way of love is called Sacrifice."[23] That is the voice of the Dove, affirming the affirmation of this world. The Christian lives between heaven and earth—not a little closer to the former so that he is so heavenly minded that he's of no earthly use, and not a little closer to the latter so that he cannot break free of the earth's gravity to have heavenly thoughts. Hugo Rahner calls it the exact midpoint, and only a man or woman whose foundation is in the reality of God "can accept and lovingly embrace the world—which includes himself—as God's handiwork, and, at the same time, toss it aside as a child would toss the toy of which it had wearied, in order then to soar upward into the 'blessed seriousness' which is God alone."[24] Such a person has taken the measure of all things from this Archimedean point and knows their value. They are enjoyable now, yes, but they are not eternally enjoyable. When the sun rises, you may extinguish the candle.

In baptism we die and rise again, recapitulating Christ's Paschal sacrifice in our own lives. That not only involves death, but also life. First we follow him into the grave: we die to self, we are taken out of the world, we are taken out of ourselves, we renounce the empty

22. Josemaría Escrivá, *The Way*, in *The Way, Furrow, The Forge* (New York: Scepter Publishers, 2013), 676.

23. Ibid., 768.

24. Hugo Rahner, *Man at Play* (New York: Herder and Herder, 1972), 40.

works and promises of Satan, we go into a watery tomb. (If you cannot remember doing it, have faith that it was done in you.) Then we follow him to his Father's house, and in this ascensional movement we bring along with us sanctified marriages, redeemed cities, evangelized cultures, and anything else Christ will need for making the new heavens and the new earth. We offer them through him, and with him, and in him, to God the almighty Father, in the unity of the Holy Spirit, for his honor and glory. The sacrifice which is offered to God the Father in Christianity is finally the whole redeemed city offering itself to its Redeemer. We are not content to merely offer bread and wine in our sacrifice; we are not content to merely offer ourselves individually; we will not be content unless the whole redeemed world is lifted up in oblation. Doing the world as it was meant to be done means doing the world as a temple in which God is glorified.

A sinner cannot sacrifice. This is what is sad about the sinner; it is a grievous thing to see. The incense will not light on coals that have been dampened by the passions; Jacob's ladder cannot be climbed if the first ascetical rung is not in place; we cannot assume the *orans* posture so long as we are bent over upon ourselves like a cripple. But through death the proper, positive relationship to the other things becomes possible. If we do not fear God, then what *do* we fear? God's will must have a true influence on our use of the world. Before we may use the world, we must leave it. This is why we associate death with sacrifice, but it is my death, not the offering's. The death of self permits affirmation of the world, and only after a positive experience of it can someone properly give it up without resentment. This is the freedom for decision that comes as a result of liturgical asceticism. The cosmos is ordered to me so that I can order it to God, and thus are all things able to attain their glorification. Remember that Coventry Patmore said sacrifice to God involves an act of faith, such as Abraham had. Like Abraham, the sinner must offer up his ruling love.

C. S. Lewis thinks that poets and artists know something about this glorification. They put the glory we are talking about into words and images and myths, because they know the question; Christianity knows the answer:

We do not want merely to see beauty, though, God knows, even that is bounty enough. We want something else which can hardly be put into words, to be united with the beauty we see, to pass into it, to receive it into ourselves, to bathe in it, to become part of it. That is why we have peopled air and earth and water with gods and goddesses and nymphs and elves that, though we cannot, yet these projections can, enjoy in themselves that beauty, grace, and power of which Nature is the image. . . . At present we are on the outside of the world, the wrong side of the door. . . . We cannot mingle with the splendors we see. But all the leaves of the New Testament are rustling with the rumor that it will not always be so. Someday, God willing, we shall get in. When human souls have become as perfect in voluntary obedience as the inanimate creation is in its lifeless obedience, then they will put on his glory, or rather that greater glory of which Nature is only the first sketch.[25]

Voluntary obedience is sacrifice perfected. It is the full-throated song of the Dove. Jesus had it; we are promised it; and the liturgy gives us the foundation from which we can move the world towards this promised glory.

The prefix "pro-" means "forward, toward," and in that sense we can understand the profane as the realm that points toward the temple. Failing this, we bend the world around ourselves instead of pointing it toward God's temple in the heavenly Jerusalem, and that is when the profane dislocates, like a bone out of the socket. That is what we have done by our sin. That is why matter does not respond to our touch and all things feel like the flamingo with which Alice tried to play croquet: they resist us. Our handling of money, sex, and beer becomes awkward because good things resist sinful use. Because the glory of God is the pre-destination of matter, material things do not work for us. We struggle with the world. But the apostolate of the laity consists of making the face of the earth a true *profanum*, re-orienting all our life to the rising sun. In the quarry of the profane we are cutting blocks for the construction of God's temple.

---

25. Lewis, "The Weight of Glory," in *The Weight of Glory*, 42–43.

We heard Augustine say that true sacrifice is anything that we do with the aim of being united to God in holy fellowship. He follows his own definition to its (theo)logical conclusion. If our body is a sacrifice when used well and chastened by temperance, how much more so the soul?, he asks. "Aflame in the fire of divine Love, and with the dross of worldly desire melted away, it is remolded into the unchangeable form of God and becomes beautiful in His sight by reason of the bounty of beauty which He has bestowed upon it."[26] How can this be? Augustine answers by turning to the practical wisdom of St. Paul when he says we must not be conformed to this world but be transformed in newness of mind (*meta-noia*). The real offering is the whole of the redeemed city, the Communion of Saints. This is sacrifice eschatologically fulfilled, says Augustine. "Such is the sacrifice of Christians: 'We, the many, are one body in Christ.' This is the Sacrifice, as the faithful understand, which the Church continues to celebrate in the sacrament of the altar, in which it is clear to the Church that she herself is offered in the very offerings she makes to God."[27] Being Church is a sacrificial act. The sacrifice is communal, it is a fellowship, it is a plural we, it is a choir, a city, an army, a flock of Doves. What sacrifice does the Church continue to celebrate at the sacred altar? She herself, offered in the offerings she makes with her Lord. Do this in the sanctuary, and the City of God will overwhelm the City of Man with the holy fire taken from the tabernacle candle that will ignite our daily life until it becomes a prayer that can rise up like incense before God. Every lifting of our hands becomes an evening offering. There is no activity in the profane world which cannot be washed and brought pure into the holy of holies and offered up with ourselves. The sacramental liturgy continues in our very person.

The liturgy does not exist for the salvation of the Church. The liturgy of the Church exists for the salvation of the world. The sacraments inside the Church are required if we are to catch sight of the sacramentality of all things outside the Church, and use all things

---

26. Augustine, *City of God*, Book X, Chapter 6 (New York: Image Books, 1958), 192–93.

27. Ibid.

outside the Church sacrificially. To perform an affirmation of images, we must be regenerated. To see the world sacramentally, as it was meant to be seen, the cataracts of the passions must be removed, our eyes enlightened, our minds illumined, our imagination reordered, our dry bones moistened, and our hearts of stone fleshed out. Then history is seen against the horizon of eternity, matter is seen sacramentally, every neighbor is an *imago Dei*, all theology is eucharistic, social justice is the radiance of the Kingdom on earth, families are *ecclesia domestica*, my sufferings are opportunities to follow Christ, the sepulcher is a birth canal. We are finally doing the world as it was meant to be done.

Appendix
Monasticism and Marriage

COMING TO THE END, I would like to return to the beginning. I began with the metaphor of a diptych because this book is connected to my earlier work on liturgical asceticism, but not the way a second volume is connected to a first. Yet a connection does exist, and they must be seen together. So I imagined a diptych with one panel portraying the silver key of negation and the other panel portraying the golden key of affirmation, hinged together by the Charles Williams quotation. The silver key makes it possible for the gold key to turn in its lock, and the gold key is the reason for the silver key's purpose.

In this appendix I would like to experiment with this thesis one more time.

In researching the ascetical tradition I stumbled across an intriguing thought repeated in both Vladimir Solovyov and Paul Evdokimov. Both men were Orthodox Christians, the former from 19th-century Russia and the latter from the 20th-century émigré population in Paris, so I was struck to find the same assertion a century apart. They said that there are two ascetical vocations: monasticism and marriage. Every baptized Christian should engage asceticism as a battle with the passions and rise toward a higher moral and spiritual life, but there are two states of life wherein this mortification is done communally. It seemed to me that these two theologians were saying that the vowed life of the monk and the vowed life of the married make their asceticism alike in some way.

Here is Solovyov's passage. He is describing our human task as one of spiritualizing the body and earthly nature in general, and this means opening our future to the resurrection. But that hopeful work requires struggle against the death that weighs upon us in the mortality of our flesh. So he writes that in our present life the necessary condition of this future perfection and the moral problem of the present state is the struggle of the spirit with the flesh, its strengthening and concentration. The present means of bodily resurrection is the subjugation of the flesh; the necessary condition of the fullness of life is asceticism.... True asceticism, i.e., spiritual power over the flesh leading to the resurrection of life, has two forms—*monasticism* and *marriage*.[1]

True marriage is the realization of the absolute moral norm and the vital center of human existence, he goes on to say, and the great mystery of every human being is realized in the ecstasy of love sanctified by the word of God. The husband therefore sees his wife "as she was from the first destined to be, as God saw her from all eternity, and as she shall be in the end."[2] The spouses see each other as they were meant to be seen, which has been our definition of mundane liturgical theology all along: in the domestic Church the man and woman do the Garden of Eden as it was meant to be done.

Evdokimov devotes an entire chapter to this idea in his book *The Sacrament of Love*, titled "Marriage and the Monastic State." He begins by reviewing Church doctrine that absolutely forbids viewing the marriage union as a defilement. Chastity is expressed not only by celibacy, it is lived in the conjugal state, too: "Chastity signifies that one belongs totally to Christ, undividedly. For monks it is an engagement of the soul in unmediated relationship, and for the spouses, engagement through the hypostasis of matrimony."[3] Therefore, Evdokimov writes that

The deepest interrelationship unites the two. The promises exchanged by the betrothed introduce them in a certain manner into a special monasticism, because here too there is a dying to the past and a rebirth into a new life.... Thus, marriage includes within

1. Vladimir Solovyov, *The Justification of the Good: An Essay on Moral Philosophy* (London: Constable and Company, 1918), 411.

2. Ibid., 416.

3. Paul Evdokimov, *The Sacrament of Love* (Crestwood, NY: St. Vladimir's Seminary Press, 1985), 67.

itself the monastic state, and that is why the latter is not a sacrament. The two converge as complementary aspects of the same virginal reality of the human spirit.[4]

What if we read monasticism in a nuptial light, and marriage in a monastic light?

A passage from Romano Guardini further convinced me that this would be possible. He provides this sketch of what it would look like:

> Marriage comprehended in the light of faith and lived in grace *becomes* "natural" in a much higher sense, as the fruit of grace, the harvest of faith. It is not beginning, but end of Christian effort, and must be formed by the same power as that behind virginity; renunciation made possible by faith. Christian marriage is constantly renewed by sacrifice. True, it fulfills and enriches the lives of both partners through fertility and a ripening of the personality beyond the limits possible for each individually; not only through the fullness and creativeness of the joint life, but also through the sacrifices necessary to weather the temptations of brute instinct, inconstancy, never-ending disappointments, moral crises, changes in fortune and the general demands of a common life.[5]

It is clear that within the daily married life there is plenty of room to exercise the Christian discipline of dying to self and rising in love to new life, which is the occupation of ascetics.

Ever since I read this provocative proposal, viz. that marriage and monasticism are twin forms of the ascetical vocation, I have wondered about exploring the connection in more detail. Perhaps it deserves a book of its own; here it receives only an appendix. I would like to experiment with the proposition by turning to a classic ascetical text, *The Ladder of Divine Ascent*, written by John Climacus, who was a seventh-century monk of St. Catherine's monastery at the base of Mount Sinai. He was a great synthesizer of the ascetical tradition that had been under development in the deserts of Palestine

---

4. Ibid., 68.
5. Romano Guardini, *The Lord* (Chicago: Henry Regnery Co., 1954), 175.

and Egypt and in the writings of theologian bishops. He constructed an account of the ascetical life by conceiving thirty steps on a ladder leading to God (hence his name, *Climacus*: of the Ladder). The book was written by a monk, for monks, and some Orthodox monks read it during every Lent in their monasteries—and yet its content contains rich insights and guidance for me, not a monk, but a married man. Can I use John Climacus to test the claim that true asceticism has two forms? Would this book for monastics have anything relevant to say to the married?

What follows does not intend to divulge my personal story, and the reader need not fear awkward or embarrassing confessions ahead. This is not a record of my ascetical-marital failures or successes because I do not want to write about myself or about my marriage (though I am drawing on more than four decades of life in the sacrament of marriage). Rather, I want write about how a monk, who lives as an icon of the silver key, can shake hands with a husband and wife, who live as an icon of the golden key. In what follows I refer to the steps in John by his chapter titles.[6]

Steps 1–3: On Renunciation and Exile

John speaks of the monastic life as a race ("If you have the fire, run...") and a pilgrimage. He speaks of the monk going into exile, exile from anything in familiar surroundings that would hinder one from attaining the ideal of holiness. The monk runs faster because he is running lighter. Chesterton said something similar about St. Francis:

> The world around him was, as has been noted, a network of feudal and family and other forms of dependence. The whole idea of St. Francis was that the Little Brothers should be like little fishes who could go freely in and out of that net. They could do so precisely because they were small fishes and in that sense even slippery

---

6. Scholars have debated over the sequence and structure of the steps, but I do not need to go into that. I will use the Paulist Press translation, *John Climacus: The Ladder*.

fishes. There was nothing that the world could hold them by; for the world catches us mostly by the fringes of our garments.[7]

In order to extol the monks' liberty, John contrasts it with the burdens carried by the person in the world. This might at first sound like he is reproaching me: "The married man is like someone chained hand and foot so when he wants to run he cannot." But it soon becomes clear that John is speaking about someone who is caught up in the affairs of the world. When the monk leaves the world, he is obeying the command Christ also gave to the married couple: be not of the world. This can be done successfully in the world so long as one is not of it. Such obedience to the kingdom of God is what the monk seeks; and, therefore, when Evdokimov wants to refer to it, he calls it "interiorized monasticism." But both he and John understand that one does not have to be a monk in order to live the kingdom. In fact, John records having been asked, "How can we who are married and living amid public cares aspire to the monastic life?"

> I answered: "Do whatever good you may. Speak evil of no one. Rob no one. Tell no lie. Despise no one and carry no hate. Do not separate yourself from the Church assemblies. Show compassion to the needy. Do not be a cause of scandal to anyone. Stay away from the bed of another, and be satisfied with what your own wives can provide you. If you do all this, you will not be far from the kingdom of heaven."

John does not recommend an ersatz monasticism to those who are married. Rather, he tells them to live their Christianity where they are. The monk is in exile from the world, but if we are talking about the world of sin, then the married Christian is every bit as much in exile. Every Christian is a fugitive from the City of Man which is ruled by Satan, and in a race to the City of God. Indeed, the question of our citizenship unfolds across our whole life, and affirming that final citizenship is the task of our asceticism.

---

7. G. K. Chesterton, *St. Francis of Assisi*, in *G. K. Chesterton Collected Works*, Vol. II (San Francisco: Ignatius Press, 1986), 93–94.

Step 4: On Obedience

Original sin entered the world by pride and was enacted as disobedience. If we are to find our way back to God we must reverse this estrangement, and that means overcoming pride; and the tool for doing so is obedience. That accounts for the special place of obedience in the monastic discipline. John writes,

> Obedience is a total renunciation of our own life, and it shows up clearly in the way we act. Or, again, obedience is the mortification of the members while the mind remains alive. Obedience is unquestioned movement, death freely accepted, simple life, danger faced without worry, an unprepared defense before God, fearlessness before death, safe voyage, sleeper's journey. Obedience is the burial place of the will and the resurrection of lowliness. . . . Indeed, to obey is, with all deliberateness, to put aside the capacity to make one's own judgment.

What are the marital vows again? Oh, yes: Love, honor, and *obey*. Does not a husband make a total renunciation of his own life in order to enter into union with his wife, and does she not do the same? Is not their obedience a burial place of an egocentric will? Putting aside the capacity to make one's own judgment does not make one into a child again, it makes a "we" out of what was formerly "my own."

The Desert Fathers loved to tell stories of radical obedience, and John includes a few himself, and the upshot of each story underscores the struggle for humility, without which there can be no true obedience. This is obedience to God, but it cannot be exercised in the abstract, it must be practiced in the concrete. If the voice we obey comes from our own mind, even if we think it to be God, then we are likely to discover it is only our own ego giving us permission to do what we wanted to do in the first place. Therefore, the monk must obey an actual person: the Abbot. And if a married Christian wants to practice obedience, he is in luck for having a partner whom he should obey. If the words which come to me never contradict my own will, then I can be pretty sure that they are my words and not God's. I need to hear the word of God in another voice—

my wife's voice, a voice that challenges my ego, that stirs my humility, that mortifies me.

Step 5: On Penitence

The life of a monk is a life of penitence, i.e., it is lived repentance. John gives the most beautiful description of repentance I have ever read when he says "Repentance is the daughter of hope and the refusal to despair. (The penitent stands guilty—but not disgraced.)" A disgraced person finds it difficult to repent. Couples who do not want to reconcile, but rather want to continue the feud, will disgrace the other when he admits his guilt. Repentance requires faith and love, that is true, but if there were no hope, we would not dare to repent. (This was the difference between Peter and Judas.) The supernatural virtue of hope makes it possible to express contrition, without which the marriage relationship could not grow. Absence of hope results in a kind of shame or self-defensiveness that frightens one from asking for forgiveness. If one refuses to ask for forgiveness (lack of hope) or the other refuses to grant forgiveness (lack of charity), then the bond is hurt. The aim of asceticism is to overcome both of these symptoms of pride. So John gives his monks encouragement: "Do not be surprised if you fall every day and do not surrender. . . . Nothing equals the mercy of God or surpasses it. To despair is therefore to inflict death on oneself. . . . Note well that we never return by the road on which we strayed, but rather by a different and a shorter route." The married couple may take equal encouragement. The deadening of a relationship happens slowly, but reconciliation can happen in a flash. The road that leads back to your beloved is shorter, and more direct, and can be more quickly traveled, than the long road which might have led to estrangement. You can mend the damage more quickly than it took to inflict it. Just do not despair. Start. Repent in hope.

Step 6: On Remembrance of Death

The wages of sin are death, and we suffer a sickness unto death. So remembrance of death is not maudlin self-despair; it is an act of facing reality. We step out of our fantasy to recognize that in our present state, without conversion, we are not fully alive. Our remembrance of death allows us to die a little bit each day, so that when we come to the grave we are well practiced in dying. Our baptismal life is a lifelong dying to sin and self and Satan. We should put our death before our minds as Jews put phylacteries upon their forehead: in order to see all experiences in the light of eternity. The husband and wife can reflect on the presence of death in a special way. They observe the cycle of life as their children are born, grow, and take up their place in the world: indeed, the passage of time is nowhere more vividly realized than watching their children grow. They watch generations pass with their own eyes. The family unit stands smack in the middle of the passage of time, and therefore John explains that the active man, as well as the contemplative monk, has things to do. "There are many things," he writes, "that the mind of a man leading the active life can do. One can think about the love of God, the remembrance of death, the remembrance of God, the remembrance of the kingdom, the seal of the holy martyrs, the remembrance of the presence of God." Such thoughts should occupy the minds of the married couple daily. All the temporal transitions they live through together should be put in the light of the eternal.

Step 7: On Mourning

John repeats the Christian idea that "the tears that come after baptism are greater than baptism itself, though it may seem rash to say so. Baptism washes off those evils that were previously within us, whereas the sins committed after baptism are washed away by tears." These spiritual tears rehydrate baptism when its water level has receded as a result of the evaporating winds of the world blowing across it. Tears are an expression of true compunction, wherein "joy and gladness mingle with what we call mourning and grief, like honey in a comb." What does a married person mourn? Harsh words and intemperate actions, pushing self to the front, foregoing the opportunities for charity that are provided daily by the marital bond. And yet gladness is mingled with those memories, because, once forgiven, these forgiven sins become the building blocks of the relationship. Mourning slows our pace so that we do not walk too brusquely past the persons of the Holy Trinity who are waiting to join us at various corners of our life.

Step 8: On Placidity and Meekness

Meekness is probably the most misunderstood word in the vocabulary of the virtues. Our culture equates meekness with spinelessness and timidity, but, to the contrary, John says meekness is "freedom from anger." Not the righteous kind of anger, but rather freedom from the kind of anger that is "an indication of concealed hatred, of grievance nursed. Anger is the wish to harm someone who has provoked you. Irascibility is an untimely flaring up of the heart. Bitterness is a stirring of the soul's capacity for displeasure." We think that we have no control over such anger—that we are provoked!—but John says "an angry person is like a voluntary epileptic." We have the convulsions involuntarily, but we have willed the disease. That is why we cannot use the excuse of no control in our marriage. "Angry people, because of their self-esteem, make a pitiable sight, though they do not realize this themselves." We have all seen bitter and bickering married couples who make pitiable sights, though they do not know it of themselves. The meekness upon which a successful marriage depends is not false humility or poor ego strength by one or the other spouse. Meekness is freedom from anger, and it is important because "there is no greater obstacle to the presence of the Spirit in us than anger." Anger at each other prevents the Spirit from entering the marriage. How to attain this meekness? The monk's practice provides useful advice: "The first step toward freedom from anger is to keep the lips silent when the heart is stirred; the next, to keep thoughts silent when the soul is upset; the last, to be totally calm when unclean winds are blowing." Overcoming anger is no easier in the monastery than in the marriage.

Step 9: On Malice

"Remembrance of wrongs comes as the final point of anger. It is a keeper of sins . . . a worm in the mind. . . . It is a pleasureless feeling cherished in the sweetness of bitterness." If one partner holds on to a wrong, or a perceived wrong, and stores its memory, bringing it out to self-justify from time to time, then free communication is dismantled. Of course wrongs will be committed; but they must be forgotten. Forgiveness and forgetting are not the same, but the latter is required if we are to move forward and build new tissue in the relationship. It is amazing how much more quickly and easily I can forget my own wrongs than another's. "Forgive quickly and you will be abundantly forgiven." Can anger in a relationship be clean and productive, rather than putrefying? Yes, but "a true sign of having completely mastered this putrefaction will come ... only when, on hearing of some catastrophe that has afflicted [another] in body or soul, you suffer and you lament for him as if for yourself." The husband and wife are asked to suffer as one, lament as one, forgive as one, grieve as one, struggle as one, proceed as one, pray as one, practice charity as one. This means letting no malicious memory of wrong divide them.

Step 10: On Slander

"I imagine that no one with any sense would dispute that slander is the child of hatred and remembrance of wrongs." If one spouse harbors a grudge, nurses a resentment, broods over past injuries, harbors and develops a secret contempt for the other, clings to a memory of being wronged, it often squirts out as slander. John says slander puts on the appearance of love, but actually it wastes and drains away the lifeblood of love, and is the ruin of chastity. Slandering another is a way of justifying oneself. The temptation to judge one's spouse is made stronger by the feeling that if I don't, who will? And we excuse ourselves for judging. Slandering one's spouse is made easier by the fact that by living together they have been able to see up close the cracks in the façade that otherwise protects the person in public. We can fool friends and business partners, but not our spouse. Unfortunately, rendering such judgment does more harm than good. Besides, we already have more than enough to do with ourselves. Concern yourself with the log in your own eye, and not the splinter in your wife's. If a person is honest, "he would feel that his time on earth did not suffice for his own mourning, even if he lived a hundred years." If you were able to see your own faults for what they are, you would not worry about anyone else in this life.

Step 11: On Talkativeness in Silence

Why worry about garrulousness? Is it only to keep quiet in the monastic refectory? No, John is censuring it for a different reason: it is simultaneously a symptom and a cause of something we must not allow to take root in a married relationship, either. Idle talkativeness is "the throne of vainglory on which it loves to preen itself and show off. Talkativeness is a sign of ignorance, a doorway to slander, a leader of jesting, a servant of lies, the ruin of compunction, a summoner of despondency, a messenger of sleep, a dissipation of recollection, the end of vigilance, the cooling of zeal, the darkening of prayer." Any of these can be damaging to the married relationship, because marriage requires times of silence in which one draws closer to one's spouse, and simultaneously draws closer to God. "Intelligent silence is the mother of prayer, freedom from bondage, custodian of zeal, a guard on our thoughts . . . the secret journey upward." There is beauty to old married couples being quiet together, made possible by a lifetime of listening.

Step 12: On Falsehood

"Lying is the destruction of charity. . . . No sensible man imagines that lying is a minor failing." A marriage cannot be built on a lie. Truthfulness is a necessary foundation for marriage. John is worried about liars in the monastery because they will break up the community; a liar will break up a marriage, too. But a married relationship shares truthfulness in one additional way: one must be truthful in body, as well. The second good of marriage is called *bonum fidei* (standing between *bonum prolis*, the good of offspring, and *bonum sacramenti*, the unbreakable bond). *Fidei*: confidence, trust, belief, faith, loyalty, honesty. It is chastity. It is being true (not false) to each other. The marriage vow says, "I promise to be true to you in good times and in bad, in sickness and in health."

Step 13: On Despondency

Despondency or tedium was known as "the noonday demon." Evagrius says this demon makes it seem that the sun barely moves at all and that the day is fifty hours long; this demon constrains the monk to look constantly out the windows and to see if perhaps some brother is coming so the regimen of prayer can be interrupted; he instills a hatred for the life in the monastery, arguing that the monk could do more good elsewhere. John takes up the same thought when he describes the consequences of tedium upon life in the monastery (laziness in the singing of psalms and weakness in prayer), and defines tedium as "a paralysis of the soul, the slackness of the mind, and neglect of religious exercises, a hostility to vows taken." If this vice of despondency takes root in marriage it will also cause a hostility to vows taken. Perhaps in marriage it is not a noon-day demon, but the proverbial seven year itch demon. A despondent dissatisfaction arises, sometimes causing a wandering eye, and one may experience hostility to the vow, once gladly professed, if one is not attentive. Chesterton observed that "In everything worth having, even in every pleasure, there is a point of pain or tedium that must be survived, so that the pleasure may revive and endure. . . . It is then that the Institution upholds a man and helps him on to the firmer ground ahead."[8] That's why we take the vow: so that there can be an Institution to uphold us when tedium strikes. We cannot make marriage rely on our mood, because we are too moody. Asceticism is a kind of support scaffolding.

Step 14: On Gluttony

It may seem that the diet in the refectory has nothing to do with the diet at the home kitchen table, but I shall try to make the case in two ways. On the one hand, John is speaking of the spiritual dimensions of gluttony: "Control your appetites before they control you." "Most food that inflates the stomach also encourages desire." This gluttony is not defined by the amount of food on the plate, but by the attitude it stimulates. "Gluttony is hypocrisy of the stomach." Some marriages are ruled by a gluttony for belongings; indeed, it seems to be a societal trend to put off marriage until one can start out at a certain expected level of luxury; and even afterward, children are delayed lest they interrupt this hypocrisy of high living. On the other hand, I do not want to overlook actual gluttony, either. John

---

8. G.K. Chesterton, *What's Wrong with the World*, in *G.K. Chesterton Collected Works*, Vol. IV (San Francisco: Ignatius Press, 1987), 69.

says, "It is truly astounding how the incorporeal mind can be defiled and darkened by the body. Equally astonishing is the fact that the immaterial spirit can be purified and refined by clay." The spiritual life shared by the husband and wife must be purified and refined by their bodies (Natural Family Planning requires a rhythmic fasting from sex). The shared practice of fasting on Fridays or during Lent brings religious commitments into the kitchen. "Lord" comes from an Anglo-Saxon word meaning *Loaf-ward*, warden of the pantry, keeper of the bread. Though no married couple fasts with the same strenuousness as the monk, I suspect John thinks that the benefits of fasting will be experienced no matter what the degree to which it is done. "Fasting makes for purity of prayer, an enlightened soul, a watchful mind, a deliverance from blindness. Fasting is the door of compunction, humble sighing, joyful contrition, an end to chatter, an occasion for silence, a custodian of obedience, a lightening of sleep, health of the body, an agent of dispassion, a remission of sins, the gate, indeed, the delight of Paradise." The Church fathers noted that the fall of our parents in Eden was caused by a kind of gluttony: the woman saw that the food was pleasing to the eyes, so she took some and ate it in an untimely manner, before it was offered by God as gift. Our battle with the consequences of that original gluttony will require a fasting by which we prove to ourselves that man does not live by bread alone.

Step 15: On Chastity

A statement was made by the Congregation for the Doctrine of the Faith on sexual ethics, called *Persona Humana* (1975). It identifies and warns against certain errors in modes of behavior, but at the end affirms that

> the virtue of chastity is in no way confined solely to avoiding the faults already listed. It is aimed at attaining higher and more positive goals. It is a virtue which concerns the whole personality, as regards both interior and outward behavior. Individuals should be endowed with this virtue according to their state in life: for some it will mean virginity or celibacy consecrated to God, which is an eminent way of giving oneself more easily to God alone with an

undivided heart. For others it will take the form determined by the moral law, according to whether they are married or single. But whatever the state of life, chastity is not simply an external state; it must make a person's heart pure. (¶11)[9]

John is going to describe the virtue of chastity as it is practiced in the celibate state of life, but chastity can also take a form determined by the married moral life.

Chastity is a pathway to the spiritual through the material; it uses a corporeal body to ascend to a spiritual excellence. "To be chaste is to put on the nature of an incorporeal being." A chaste man uses "heavenly fire to quench the fires of the flesh." John, addressing a monastery, will speak of quenching the fires; addressing a marriage, we will speak of the right use of the fire. The sexual appetite is given by God, and therefore good, but justice always involves using a good at the right time, in the right way, in the right measure, for the right reason, with the right person, and so forth. The apostle Paul spoke of the conflict between "the law of his mind" and the "law of sin which dwells in his members" (Romans 7:23). John picks up this thought when he speaks of chastity as mastering one's body and taking command of nature. We must take command of nature, rather than allowing the law of sin to do so. Our battle is not with the body, as if the material body was wicked (in some Manichaean sense); our battle is with the spiritual demons. "That spirit should fight with spirit is not surprising. The real wonder is that a man dwelling in his body, and always struggling against this hostile and canny matter, should manage to rout spiritual foes." The battle is not with the body, but it takes place in the body, and by the right use of the body we can rout sin. The husband and wife have been called to this same fight, and they conduct it by having been made one flesh. They make a bodily attainment of chastity, which is the opposite of impurity, says John. *Persona Humana* says, "this virtue increases the human person's dignity and enables him to love truly, disinterestedly, unselfishly and with respect for others" (¶12). Chastity is the

---

9. http://www.vatican.va/roman_curia/congregations/cfaith/documents/rc_co n_cfaith_doc_19751229_persona-humana_en.html

opposite of inauthentic love. To love my wife disinterestedly means not using her as a means to my own end, but to love her for herself, as herself.

Step 18: On Insensitivity

Perhaps the most frequent accusation made in a failing marriage is that one partner was insensitive to the other. What is an insensitive man like? John says he is "a foolish philosopher ... a blind man teaching sight to others. He talks about healing a wound and does not stop making it worse. He complains about what has happened and does not stop eating what is harmful." I imagine these very words occurring in any marriage counselor's office. John thinks insensitivity is a deadened feeling that comes from long carelessness. "It is thought gone numb, an offspring of predisposition, a trap for zeal, a noose for courage, an ignorance of compunction, the gateway to despair...." John is, of course, talking about monks who are fulfilling their vows inattentively, for whom love has become rule-keeping, and care has become thoughtless. They say one thing but do another, they do one thing but say another; they are hypocrites. Such hypocrisy does not bode well for a marriage, either. Husband and wife must be sensitive to one another, and their love must not become a matter of rule-keeping, either. The laws of the vow are not meant to replace love, they are meant to keep love live. John describes a series of insensitive inconsistencies in the monastery: someone blesses silence but cannot stop talking about it, teaches meekness and gets angry while teaching it, criticizes himself for being vainglorious and looks around for glory for making the admission, etc. A similar list of insensitive inconsistencies could be drawn up in the home: someone praises the domestic life but spends no time there, teaches docility but puffs himself up while teaching it, criticizes himself for being selfish and looks around for a reward.

Step 19: On Sleep, Prayer, and the Singing in Church of Psalms

This very short chapter primarily deals with monks making it out of bed in time for morning prayer, but it does remind me that husband and wife have the privilege of falling asleep and waking up together. "Sleep is a natural state. It is also an image of death and a respite of the senses." The Christian tradition has long compared sleep to death, because in both—one in a minor and one in a major way—we must relinquish our jurisdiction and fall into trustful dependence. The husband and wife have the honor of practicing this together. Catholic prayers for the family have brought forward this symbolism of death: "Awake may we watch with Christ, and asleep may we rest in peace." A married couple shares the actions of eating and talking and working and playing; they also share the act of sleep. It, too, can be made a religious occasion.

Step 20: On Alertness

John is speaking here of alertness through nighttime vigils: "Monks collect their wealth and knowledge during the hours of evening and night when they are standing at prayer and contemplation." Many of the Sayings of the Desert Fathers laud the monk who does without sleep. Arsenius said, "One hour's sleep is enough for a monk if he is a fighter."[10] They were hurrying out of this world, so they resisted all biological needs: food, sex, and sleep. I believe we might flip this one on its head. I tell my students that it would be an ascetical accomplishment for them to sleep not one hour, but eight. To have a full night's sleep what must they do? Cancel activities, be diligent with the use of their daylight hours, ascetically restrain themselves from over-commitment. It is only vainglory that makes us think that some group can't get along without us. Or perhaps we should not flip this one for the married couple but leave it as a challenge: if they manage to stay up for the late, late show, couldn't they manage a night vigil of Psalms?

Step 21: On Unmanly Fears

Some marriages fail from fear, and the couple needs to be more stalwart. Asceticism is a system for practicing strength training. John writes, "Fear is danger tasted in advance, a quiver as the heart takes fright before unnamed calamity. Fear is a loss of assurance." Fear

10. The Sayings of the Desert Fathers, IV.3. See Benedicta Ward, *The Desert Fathers: Sayings of the Early Christian Monks* (New York: Penguin Books, 2003).

makes us unsure that we can keep the vow; our imagination pictures calamities befalling one mate that will inconvenience the other; we taste dangers in the relationship that have not yet happened. We frequently act cowardly out of vaingloriousness. This fear has an air of unreality because it is found not in the present but in the as yet unrealized future. "Cowardice is childish behavior within the soul advanced in years and vainglory. It is a lapse from faith that comes from anticipating the unexpected." Marriage should be an adventure; you cannot remain in the fetal position forever.

Step 22: On Vainglory

The ascetical tradition makes a distinction between pride and vainglory that took me a long time to understand. Pride concerns our relationship with God, and is an attempt to break out of dependence upon him in order to run our own lives. Vainglory is seeking the praise of other human beings. When that praise is deserved, it is not in vain. But when it is not deserved, then expecting it from your husband or wife will irritate them. The vainglorious person is swelled up, notices himself, and takes note of criticism, says John. This is hard to live with. And it is difficult to overcome. "Vainglory beams on every occupation. . . . I fast, and turn vainglorious. I stop fasting so that I will draw no attention to myself, and I become vainglorious over my prudence. I dress well or badly, and am vainglorious in either case. I talk or I hold my peace, and each time I am defeated." The beginning stage, therefore, is to remain silent and accept dishonor gladly; the middle stage is to check every vainglory while it is still in thought; the end stage is "to be able to accept humiliation before others without actually feeling it." Overcoming vainglory will feel like we are being belittled, but it is not so; we are simply finding our correct size in the universe. Humility is not the attempt to hold a low opinion of yourself, it is the attempt to hold a correct opinion of yourself. Asceticism must disable vainglory, and God has given husbands wives to help with the process.

Step 23: On Pride

If vainglory vexes the horizontal relationship between husband and wife, the appearance of pride on the scene is worse because it cripples our vertical relationship with God, and so dries up the supply of power to the virtues. "Pride is a denial of God, an invention of the devil, contempt for men. It is the mother of condemnation, the offspring of praise, a sign of barrenness. It is a flight from God's help." Who can be healed if he flees the Divine Therapist? God does not forbid pride because he is being offended, he forbids it because it is a false situation: it makes us believe that God is not God, the source of all things. Pride is blasphemy. No, worse: pride is idolatry. Pride attempts to put oneself in charge of the universe, when, in fact, John says with a smile on his lips that all things are a gift from God. "You may be proud only of the achievements you had before the time of your birth. But anything after that, indeed the birth itself, is a gift from God." He ends this step on the ladder with the story of a zealous monk who wore himself out for twenty years with fasting and vigils attempting to overcome this demon of pride, but to no avail. His actions fed his pride. So he went to an old man for advice, and the old man told him, "My son, put your hand on my neck. . . . Now let this sin be on my neck for as many years as it has been or will be active within you." (Even before the young monk left the cell of this old man, his infirmity was gone.) Husbands and wives will do the same. One will take on the difficulty for the sake of healing the other. Some things we cannot do for ourselves, we must be joined (*conjugalis*) to another; any progress we make is a gift from another, if we will not be too proud to accept.

Step 24: On Meekness, Simplicity, Guilelessness, and Wickedness

We are nearing the top of the ladder. The next three virtues—simplicity, humility, and discernment—belong to the higher virtues of the active life, and the final four—stillness, prayer, dispassion, and love—are a transition to the contemplative life.

In speaking of simplicity, John returns to the theme of meekness, and I'm sure it would sound startling to suggest that a marriage would thrive better if the partners were meek. According to our modern understanding, a meek woman is deferential to the point of losing her personality, and a meek man is a timid milquetoast. But John says "Meekness is a rock looking out over the sea of anger which breaks the waves which come crashing on it and stays entirely unmoved. Meekness is the bulwark of patience, the door, indeed the mother of love." If we are not meek, self-defensive anger flares up and we cannot admit our faults. If we attain meekness, then simplicity stands against wickedness and guile, against the calculating soul, against malice and false heart. This imitates Christ. Meekness does not mean being unmoved, in the sense of lacking sympathy or compassion; it means forgoing movements of anger and irritation that arise from within. "Meekness is a mind consistent amid honor or dishonor." It is a power, the power to act charitably toward another even if one feels jibed at. To overcome a stalemate, usually the husband or the wife, one or the other, must take the higher, meeker ground and make a gesture that is not a reprisal. One or the other must let the waves of anger break without mounting a counterattack. One or the other must be meek. You may take turns.

Step 25: On Humility

"Humility is constant forgetfulness of one's achievements." How does one forget one's achievements in marriage? When they are no longer "mine," but "ours"; when two have become one, and there is no longer my accomplishment, my achievement, my reward, my honor; when whatever comes from the outside world passes through one to shine on the other because they share a spiritual transparency. John records some other definitions. Humility is the admission that "one is the least important and is also the greatest sinner"; "it is the mind's awareness that one is weak and helpless"; "it is to be the first to end a quarrel." That last is a handy skill to bring to a marriage. One of my favorite stories from the Desert Fathers is about two old men who had lived together in one cell and

never had there arisen even the paltriest contention between them. So the one said to the other, "Let us have one quarrel the way other men do." But the other said, "I do not know how one makes a quarrel." The first said, "Look, I set the tile between us and say, 'That is mine,' and you say, 'It is not thine, it is mine.' And thence arises contention and the squabble." So they set the tile between them, and the first one said, "That is mine," and the second made reply: "I hope that it is mine." And the first said, "It is not thine: it is mine." To which the second made answer, "If it is thine, take it." After which they could find no way of quarreling.[11]

Two married souls in such a state could find no way of quarreling. Imagine.

John adds that humility "is the acknowledgment of divine grace and divine mercy." In marriage this divine mercy is communicated through another human being in such a way that when my wife is merciful I know that it is God being merciful. That is what makes the marriage a sacrament. The marriage is sacramental because each spouse is an encounter with divine grace for the other. This humility involves a real repentance, which John says is even a sort of mingling with God. But it must be true humility, not faux, and so it is good to have another rod to compare against, like a family. "The solitary horse can often imagine itself to be at full gallop, but when it finds itself in a herd it then discovers how slow it actually is." We would benefit from having a measure of our virtues, which would reveal secret corners where humility has not yet reached. "Most of us would describe ourselves as sinners. And perhaps we really think so. But it is indignity that shows up the true state of the heart." The person who knows which buttons to push will show up the true state of the heart. So long as there is an ounce of ego, humility will feel like humiliation.

If one were serious about seeking deification, one would be grateful for each practice session of humility. "Because of our unwillingness to humble ourselves, God has arranged that no one can see his own faults as clearly as his neighbor does. Hence our obligation to be grateful not to ourselves but to our neighbor and to God for our healing." The person to whom we should be most grateful for our healing is the person who knows where the faults are. That's why there is more power—and more risk—for deification in marriage than in any other relationship. It is not just a matter of mind; it is a matter of practice. "The Lord understood that the virtue of the soul

11. I am using Helen Waddell's translation, *The Desert Fathers* (Ann Arbor: University of Michigan Press, 1936), 142.

is shaped by our outward behavior. He therefore took a towel and showed us how to walk the road of humility (John 13:4). The soul indeed is molded by the doings of the body." In marriage two bodies are united and can train for humility.

Step 26: On Discernment

"Discernment is a solid understanding of the will of God in all times, in all places, in all things." Surely this is not a goal of monks alone; every Christian wishes to possess this discernment. Husbands and wives discover the will of God together; they share discernment. Then a God-directed conscience becomes their "aim and rule and everything so that, knowing how the wind is blowing, we may set our sails accordingly." Where is your life going? Where do you want your family to end up? Set your sail accordingly. John identifies plenty of pitfalls dug by the demons, and the husband and wife must be careful not to fall into them. The demons impede worthwhile achievement, they distract us to things not according to the will of God, they praise us so that we become careless in our pride, they stir up sudden anger, or hopelessness, or despair, or ignorance. As we near the top of the ladder we must be ever more alert. It is easy to be attentive to rudimentary pious actions when marriage is on the lower rungs of the ladder, like grace before meals and attendance at Mass; it becomes more challenging in the elevated air near the top of the ladder. How will husband and wife express spirituality toward each other? How will they construct their common spirituality? It will be unique to each couple. "There are many roads to holiness—and to hell. A path wrong for one will suit another, yet what each is doing is pleasing to God." This means that there is no simple, one size fits all spirituality. It must be constructed over the course of a lifetime. But on what else should we spend our time?

A Summary

John interrupts himself to give a summary of the steps so far, before getting to the final four. In this penultimate review he says some clarifying things for our thesis, like "Love of God is the foundation of exile." The reason for the exile he spoke about in the first chapters is for increasing one's love for God. That reason applies equally to the monastery and the home, though it is worked out differently in each. This summary interlude is filled with pithy statements—almost fortune-cookie style. Many of them describe monastics, but do not the following describe certain saints you have met in your life? "A wearer of perfume is detected, whether he wishes it or not, by the aromas around him. A carrier of God's Spirit is detected in his speech and in his lowliness." "A dead man cannot walk. A man in despair cannot be saved." "One spark has often set fire to a great forest, and it has been found that one good deed can wipe away a multitude of sins." "A man eager for salvation thinks of death and the judgment in the same way that a starving man thinks of bread." That last one explains a lot about the monastic existence, but a secular Christian should be equally eager for salvation, and he must equally pass through death and judgment to reach it.

Most of all this final summary encourages monks to persevere. The arrow nears the target, so don't swerve now. He recites a string of cause and effect sayings (so again resorts to the mother and child metaphor):

> The offspring of virtue is perseverance. The fruit and offspring of perseverance is habit, and the child of habit is character. Good character begets fear, fear begets observance of the commandments . . . to keep the commandments is to show love, and the starting point of love is an abundance of humility, which in turn is the daughter of dispassion. To have dispassion is to have the fullness of love, by which I mean the complete indwelling of God.

Perseverance and integrity are necessities in a vowed state. Without them, we lapse. But John does not press perseverance upon us by telling us to suffer through the consequences of our promises with a stiff upper lip. Rather, he sees perseverance as a stalk which connects the roots of virtue with the fruit of love. Blessed are the pure in heart, for they shall see God (Matthew 5:8), and purity of heart is to will one thing, namely God, which means overcoming the temptation of distraction. Having wife and property and responsibilities and children need not distract us from God, but it is possible to let them do so if we have not integrated our daily life into our quest for

God, and if we do not have eyes to see the Father summoning us in every opportunity to take up a cross and follow his Son into the heart of love. John actually believes that "We can learn to perceive intelligible things clearly by means of every thing that exists in the natural world."

Step 27: On Stillness

In the ascetical tradition this stillness was referred to as hesychasm, and monks were called hesychasts, from *hesychia*, meaning stillness, rest, quiet, silence. It is a mystical quiet, an accomplishment of the heart, which means that although a monk may do this on the outside, the married should do this on the inside: "Stillness of the body is the accurate knowledge and management of one's feelings and perceptions. Stillness of soul is the accurate knowledge of one's thoughts and is an unassailable mind." Hesychasm is finding the still point at the center of a daily gyration. It is space for self-consciousness, self-attentiveness, self-awareness, not in order to be egocentric but in order to have a self sufficiently integrated so that we have a self to share. The husband should give his wife himself, not only things, and not only activities. The location of this hesychastic silence is the heart, and when we say that we "love someone with our whole heart," we are referring to the integrity produced by hesychasm. What asceticism does is to form that heart so we can love with it.

This silence is a result of overcoming the passions, and it is necessary for prayer. "It is risky to swim in one's clothes. A slave of passion should not dabble in theology." I keep that saying above my desk.

Like the prophets sometimes acted out their prophecy (Hosea married a harlot so he could experience what God felt from Israel's infidelity), some monks act out their hesychasm by becoming solitaries, and John turns his attention to them. He observes that they have various motives, but standing behind them all must be a delight in, and a thirst for, the love and sweetness of God. The hermit cannot be a masochist or a misanthrope. He achieves the union he seeks only after he has shed all despondency. "The man who is ill-tempered and conceited, hypocritical and a nurse of grievances, ought never to enter the life of solitude." Only the man who enters stillness for good reason will discover it benefits him. "Stillness is worshiping God unceasingly and waiting on Him."

What would absence of stillness in the family look like? Commotion, talk without communication, turmoil in emotion, upheaval in relationship, busyness without direction, not waiting on others (both in the sense of patience and in the sense of serving), and definitely not waiting on God. The hesychasm in the home is not as constant as the hesychasm of the hermit, but if it does not happen sometimes, and regularly, the noise of life will drown out the still, small voice of God for which the family should be listening. John describes the pathetic sight of a monk who is unfaithful to his hesychasm (forgetfulness of death, an insatiable belly, eyes out of control, vainglory at work, a calloused heart, spiritual upheaval, argumentativeness, attachment to things, doubt, talkativeness) and says its most serious symptom is a heart without compunction. A test for stillness in a married relationship would involve testing the sensitivity of one's conscience.

Step 28: On Prayer

It is ironic that we so easily believe that prayer should belong both to the monastery and the home, but do not see that the ascetical preparation for prayer belongs as much to the latter as to the former.

"Prayer is by nature a dialogue and a union of man with God. Its effect is to hold the worlds together. . . . Prayer is the mother and daughter of tears. . . . Prayer is future gladness, action without end, wellspring of virtues, source of grace, hidden progress, food of the soul, enlightenment of the mind, an axe against despair, hope demonstrated, sorrow done away with." Marriage must be a prayer. More than just praying during a marriage, the marriage itself must become a prayer. This is lived liturgy: a husband and wife as lived prayer. John says prayer is of three kinds, and should come in this sequence: heartfelt thanksgiving, confession/genuine contrition of soul, and then our request to the universal king. This is a rhythmic structure to prayer. John advises us not to talk excessively in our prayer, because then our mind is distracted by the search for words. If we have attained the stillness of step 27, the prayer of step 28 will come more easily. Just train the mind not to wander. It will wander into all kinds of worldly concerns (including valid and worthwhile concerns), which is why John calls prayer "a turning away from the world" and a clinging to God undistractedly. It is difficult because our mind moves so rapidly. St. Bonaventure once met a peasant who claimed he could pray with total concentration, so the saint said if he could pray the Lord's Prayer and think of nothing else, he would give the peasant his horse, and before the man got to "who art in heaven" he wondered if that meant the saddle, too.

Sometimes prayer is easy, but that is usually because we want something; desiring something for ourselves tends to focus the mind. Expanding our prayer beyond its egocentric boundaries requires some work. Do not worry if it is hard work, and do not worry if you sometimes fail. Even failures will work toward your growth. "Hold on to the staff of prayer and you will not fall. And even a fall will not be fatal, since prayer is a devout coercion of God" (the persistent widow in Luke 18:5). The fullness of prayer must be taught by God himself. "You cannot learn to see just because someone tells you to do so. . . . In the same way, you cannot discover from the teaching of others the beauty of prayer. Prayer has its own special teacher in God." It is a miraculous thing to be taught prayer, but the joy is doubled when husband and wife are conjugated. They can each share their unique spiritual beauty with the other. Prayer is deeply personal, but husband and wife risk sharing with each other what the Divine Pedagogue is teaching them.

Step 29: On Dispassion

"By dispassion I mean a heaven of the mind within the heart," John says. The Greek word is *apatheia*, which means not being afflicted by the passions of the vices. It is being calm and untroubled by the demons. It is the state that Evagrius's pupil, John Cassian, translated as "purity of heart," which Jesus says in the Beatitudes means seeing God. It is having overcome gluttony, lechery, cupidity, despondency, vainglory, and pride. Would not such freedom be necessary in order for love to flourish between two people? Freedom from the passions (vices) is necessary for the passion (intense intimacy) of love to flourish, because how else can we give ourselves unstintingly, limitlessly? So John tells us to think of dispassion as a kind of celestial palace—indeed, the bridal chamber of the palace. Dispassion has built its walls against the vices so that within the bridal chamber we may have peaceful and intimate communion with God, who himself is not selfish, and joyfully invites us to join him, two by two.

Step 30: On Faith, Hope, and Love

We speak of "falling in love" because there is a certain helplessness in the experience. John also describes love as "an inebriation of the soul," but he does so when he is describing love's activity. When love rules us we are inebriated and do not hinder ourselves from acting for the good of the other. God does this all day long, and "Love, by its nature, is a resemblance to God, insofar as this is humanly possible." To love is to want the good of the other, and to work for the good of the other. God does this within himself in the Trinity, and he does this outside himself in Creation. The shadows of the passions block some part of the full light of love from shining on another, but as asceticism mops up those shadows the brilliance of love increases. Jesus made marriage a sacrament (efficacious sign) of the Church because the kind of love attained in marriage is a model of the sort of love we want to attain in our religion. "Lucky the man who loves and longs for God as a spirit and lover does for his beloved. . . . Someone truly in love keeps before his mind's eye the face of the beloved and embraces it there tenderly." John uses an example from infatuated married love to describe what the monk aims at. On the final step of the ladder, he uses an example from corporeal love to paint a picture of spiritual love. "Even during sleep the longing continues unappeased, and he murmurs to his beloved. That is how it is for the body. And that is how it is for the spirit." On the final step of the ladder, he describes the love of God by referring to the effects of human love. "If the sight of the one we love clearly makes us change completely, so that we turn cheerful, glad, and carefree, what will the face of the Lord Himself not do as He comes to dwell, invisibly, in a pure soul?" When the Lord himself dwells in the husband, and dwells in the wife, they become the Lord's face to each other, to their children, and to the world. They will beam with the light of heaven. Their marriage will be a refraction of grace, bending the light of glory to shine on one particular, holy habitation.

Here ends my experiment; I try to create an image in your mind in closing.

One of the most interesting characters created by C. S. Lewis in his *Chronicles of Narnia* is a mouse named Reepicheep. He figures in two stories, and in every appearance he confirms by action and word that he is a mouse of great honor. Lewis has made him a chivalrous knight (minus the armor) because it is amusing to see a heart the size of a lion fitted into a body the size of a mouse's. In the battle Prince Caspian wages against his tyrant uncle, Reepicheep wields his sword more bravely than anyone else, though it costs him his tail and Aslan must regrow it. And on the Dawn Treader's voyage in search of the seven lost lords, Reepicheep is more loyal to Prince Caspian than any crew member, and his bravery often inspires them all to achieve things they did not expect they could. When the crew threatens mutiny, Reepicheep quietly says,

> My own plans are made. While I can, I sail east in the Dawn Treader. When she fails me, I paddle east in my coracle. When she sinks, I shall swim east with my four paws. And when I can swim no longer, if I have not reached Aslan's country, or shot over the edge of the world in some vast cataract, I shall sink with my nose to the sunrise and Peepiceek will be head of the talking mice in Narnia.[12]

Forward they sail. Eastward. On and on, to the east. In excitement Reepicheep discovers that the water has turned sweet, which he takes as evidence that they near the eastern edge of the world, as said in a nursery rhyme he learned as a young mouse pup. And then the Dawn Treader sails into a Lake of Lilies which is so shallow that the ship can go no further, and there occur two clashes between Reepicheep and his King. The mouse acts upon his previously stated intention to lower his coracle and paddle to the utter east, and Caspian announces he intends to accompany the mouse, handing com-

---

12. *Voyage of the Dawn Treader*, in *The Chronicles of Narnia* (New York: Harper-Collins Publishers, 2001), 524.

mand of the ship over to the first mate. Reepicheep objects, as do all the others. If anyone else did this, it would be called deserting. Reepicheep calls the captain to his senses: "You are the King of Narnia. You break faith with all your subjects . . . if you do not return. You shall not please yourself with adventures as if you were a private person. And if your Majesty will not hear reason, it will be the truest loyalty of every man on board to follow me in disarming and binding you till you come to your senses."[13] Feeling himself undone in argument, Caspian orders in bad temper that the ship reverse course and they will all return home. And here comes the second clash with Reepicheep. He politely says that they do not *all* return, for he still intends to go forward. "Silence!" thunders Caspian. "I've been lessoned but I'll not be baited. Will no one silence that Mouse?"[14]

The conflict between the mouse and his King is resolved by the appearance of Aslan in the privacy of the King's cabin. The gold lion's head on the wall comes to life and speaks to him, with terrible eyes, saying that Reepicheep and the three children are to go on, and he, the King, is to go back. Alone, and at once.

I will not spoil the ending for those who haven't read it, having enough here to make my point. Louis Bouyer describes the Christian life as one animated by a movement, an impulse, which can only be described as "ascensional." Christ has penetrated to the highest heavens, into the Holy of Holies, and every baptism is another person joining Christ in his ascending journey. Every paschal mystery celebrates this exodus, this exile. Christ is the first to journey this passage from earth to heaven, but he is not the last: he is the first born of many brothers and sisters who become fellow travelers. Christ puts our feet back on a heaven-directed path, and provides them vigor. Now, Bouyer says that in its ascensional movement the human spirit is to embrace matter once more and establish it in the cosmic eucharistic cycle. The cosmic priesthood will offer up creation to its source, and thus the world will finally be liberated from death by one who is the very child of the earth (Jesus has become a son of Adam). Bouyer writes,

13. Ibid., 537.
14. Ibid., 538.

The redeemed, once they have crossed the river of baptism, move upward to the city in a white throng. This company, ecstatically echoing the timeless adoration of the hypercosmic powers in hymns to their newly-won salvation, mounts up towards Christ, the cornerstone, meeting place of heaven and earth, of the Church of the firstborn whose names are written in heaven and the Church of the redeemed on earth.[15]

The fulfillment of this ascensional transfer of earthly and temporal goods to the throne of God where it can participate in cosmic liturgy waits for eschatological completion. It will not be complete until the last day, but there are some who run ahead. Bouyer says, "The monastery is simply the apex of the pilgrim Church. Or, if you prefer, it is the anticipated realization of its eternal destiny. And it is so because, like the heavenly city, it is essentially a choir of adoration, a liturgical society."[16] The monk is living the angelic life already, for here the monk does what the angels in heaven do: nothing but praise.

Now we can finally put the question of the relationship between monk and married Christian correctly: *would Caspian blame Reepicheep for going on? Would Reepicheep blame Caspian for going back?*

Caspian, the secular Christian, has work to do at Cair Paravel. He sits on a throne; he rules in the name of the Emperor Beyond the Sea; he is not "a private person." The secular baptized Christian in the world is a public person, with the dignity of naming the animals (Genesis 2), being steward of creation, serving the Kingdom's advance as it restores the world to radical justice. Caspian cannot go where the monk goes; he is not supposed to. But he need not retard Reepicheep. Some run on ahead. They are called by Aslan, and the monk would be disobedient if he did not leave this world early. One day the secular Christian will leave this world, too (when he dies). Caspian and Reepicheep will arrive in the same place, but at different times. In his vows, the monk drops everything that would slow him down; he runs faster by the vow of poverty and celibacy. But

15. Louis Bouyer, *The Meaning of the Monastic Life*, 36–37.
16. Ibid.

the many will arrive at the same place, by and by, and along the way their task is to gather up creation. It is why they walk more slowly. They arrive at the same place, but they are carrying with them sanctified marriages, redeemed cities, evangelized philosophies, and all the raw material out of which Christ will make the new heavens and new earth.

There is, therefore, no competition between the private person and the public person, between the monk and the married and the ordained priest (but that third category is for yet another essay). They are each following their path. I do not benefit myself by slowing Reepicheep down; I do not honor my position by flattening out the communion of saints; I do not feel guilty when my Lenten fast does not match the athletic performance of the desert hermit; and I do not need to assuage my guilt by suggesting the monk lighten up. Indeed, the monk's asceticism inspires mine, even while it is not for me to keep in the same way. There is a liturgical theology to do in the sanctuary, there is also a mundane liturgical theology to do in the world. The first is form of the substance, the second is matter of the substance. There is monastic asceticism to do in the monastery, there is also secular asceticism to do in the world. The commands of Christ bear equal weight on all his children, though their measure and implementation bows down in imitation of his kenosis to suit the needs of place and person.

About the Author

DAVID W. FAGERBERG is Professor in the Department of Theology at the University of Notre Dame. He holds an M.Div. from Luther Northwestern Seminary; an M.A. from St. John's University, Collegeville; an S.T.M. from Yale Divinity School; and the Ph.D. from Yale University. His work has focused upon how the Church's *lex credendi* (law of belief) is founded upon the Church's *lex orandi* (law of prayer). He has treated this in *Theologia Prima* (Hillenbrand Books, 2003) and numerous articles. Into this he has integrated the Orthodox understanding of asceticism, as preparing the liturgical person, in *On Liturgical Asceticism* (Catholic University Press, 2013). He also has an avocation in G. K. Chesterton, having published *The Size of Chesterton's Catholicism* (University of Notre Dame, 1998) and *Chesterton is Everywhere* (Emmaus Press, 2013).

Made in the USA
Las Vegas, NV
23 December 2023

83470470R00092